Russian and East European Books and Manuscripts in the United States

Proceedings of a Conference in Honor of the Fiftieth Anniversary of the Bakhmeteff Archive of Russian and East European History and Culture

Russian and East European Books and Manuscripts in the United States: Proceedings of a Conference in Honor of the Fiftieth Anniversary of the Bakhmeteff Archive of Russian and East European History and Culture has been co-published simultaneously as *Slavic & East European Information Resources,* Volume 4, Number 4 2003.

Slavic & East European Information Resources Monographic "Separates"

Below is a list of "separates," which in serials librarianship means a special issue simultaneously published as a special journal issue or double-issue *and* as a "separate" hardbound monograph. (This is a format which we also call a "DocuSerial.")

"Separates" are published because specialized libraries or professionals may wish to purchase a specific thematic issue by itself in a format which can be separately cataloged and shelved, as opposed to purchasing the journal on an on-going basis. Faculty members may also more easily consider a "separate" for classroom adoption.

"Separates" are carefully classified separately with the major book jobbers so that the journal tie-in can be noted on new book order slips to avoid duplicate purchasing.

You may wish to visit Haworth's website at . . .

http://www.HaworthPress.com

. . . to search our online catalog for complete tables of contents of these separates and related publications.

You may also call 1-800-HAWORTH (outside US/Canada: 607-722-5857), or Fax 1-800-895-0582 (outside US/Canada: 607-771-0012), or e-mail at:

docdelivery@haworthpress.com

Russian and East European Books and Manuscripts in the United States: Proceedings of a Conference in Honor of the Fiftieth Anniversary of the Bakhmeteff Archive of Russian and East European History and Culture, edited by Tanya Chebotarev and Jared S. Ingersoll (Vol. 4, No. 4, 2003). *This book documents the concerted effort to preserve Russian and East European written culture outside the bounds of Communist power.*

Judaica in the Slavic Realm, Slavica in the Judaic Realm: Repositories, Collections, Projects, Publications, edited by Zachary M. Baker, MA (Vol. 4, No. 2/3, 2003). *A collection of essays, bibliographies, and research studies illustrating the state of Jewish-related publishing ventures in Eastern Europe and the former Soviet Union, and documenting efforts by Judaic scholars, librarians, and genealogists to provide access to archival collections in those countries.*

Libraries in Open Societies: Proceedings of the Fifth International Slavic Librarians' Conference, edited by Harold M. Leich, MLS (Vol. 3, No. 2/3, 2002). *"The papers collected in this book are not only the product of this international conference, but also are concrete evidence of how far Slavic librarianship has progressed over the past 30 years. Valuable–not only to those with an interest in the Slavic field but to any librarian with an interest in area studies librarianship, international networking, and collection development." (Robert H. Burger, PhD, MLS, former Head of the Slavic and East European Library, University of Illinois at Urbana-Champaign)*

Publishing in Yugoslavia's Successor States, edited by Michael Biggins, PhD, MS, and Janet Crayne, MLIS, MA (Vol. 1, No. 2/3, 2000). *"A valuable tool, one which has been sorely lacking. All regions of the area are covered. The list of vendors, most with contact information that includes Web sites, will certainly be of service to those charged with acquiring these publications. An indispensible resource for anyone needing access to the publications of this region." (Allan Urbanic, PhD, MLIS, Librarian for Slavic Collections, University of California, Berkeley)*

Russian and East European Books and Manuscripts in the United States

Proceedings of a Conference in Honor of the Fiftieth Anniversary of the Bakhmeteff Archive of Russian and East European History and Culture

Tanya Chebotarev
Jared S. Ingersoll
Editors

Russian and East European Books and Manuscripts in the United States: Proceedings of a Conference in Honor of the Fiftieth Anniversary of the Bakhmeteff Archive of Russian and East European History and Culture has been co-published simultaneously as *Slavic & East European Information Resources,* Volume 4, Number 4 2003.

The Haworth Information Press®
An Imprint of The Haworth Press, Inc.

New York • London • Victoria (AU)
www.HaworthPress.com

Published by

The Haworth Information Press®, 10 Alice Street, Binghamton, NY 13904-1580 USA

The Haworth Information Press® is an imprint of The Haworth Press, Inc., 10 Alice Street, Binghamton, NY 13904-1580 USA.

Russian and East European Books and Manuscripts in the United States: Proceedings of a Conference in Honor of the Fiftieth Anniversary of the Bakhmeteff Archive of Russian and East European History and Culture has been co-published simultaneously as *Slavic & East European Information Resources,* Volume 4, Number 4 2003.

The development, preparation, and publication of this work has been undertaken with great care. However, the publisher, employees, editors, and agents of The Haworth Press and all imprints of The Haworth Press, Inc., including The Haworth Medical Press® and The Pharmaceutical Products Press®, are not responsible for any errors contained herein or for consequences that may ensue from use of materials or information contained in this work. Opinions expressed by the author(s) are not necessarily those of The Haworth Press, Inc. With regard to case studies, identities and circumstances of individuals discussed herein have been changed to protect confidentiality. Any resemblance to actual persons, living or dead, is entirely coincidental.

Cover design by Marylouise Doyle.

Library of Congress Cataloging-in-Publication Data

Russian and East European books and manuscripts in the United States: proceedings of a conference in honor of the fiftieth anniversary of the Bakhmeteff Archive of Russian and East European History and Culture / Tanya Chebotarev, Jared S. Ingersoll, editors.
     p. cm.
     "Co-published simultaneously as 'Slavic & East European information resources'; vol. 4, no. 4, 2003."
     Includes bibliographical references.
     ISBN 0-7890-2404-7 (hard cover: alk. paper) – ISBN 0-7890-2405-5 (soft cover: alk. paper)
     1. Bakhmeteff Archive of Russian and East European History and Culture–Congresses. 2. Bakhmetev, B. A. (Boris Aleksandrovich)–Influence–Congresses. 3. Russia–History–Archival resources–United States–Congresses. 4. Russia (Federation)–History–Archival resources–United States–Congresses. 5. Soviet Union–History–Archival resources–United States–Congresses. 6. Europe, Eastern–History–20th century–Archival resources–United States–Congresses. 7. Archival resources–United States–Congresses. 8. Exiles–United States–Archival resources–Congresses. 9. Political refugees–United States–Archival resources–Congresses. I. Ingersoll, Jared S. II. Chebotarev, Tanya. III. Bakhmeteff Archive of Russian and East European History and Culture. IV. Slavic & East European information resources. V. Title.

CD1739.N483B35 2004
026'.947'000973–dc22
                                        2003017537

Indexing, Abstracting & Website/Internet Coverage

This section provides you with a list of major indexing & abstracting services. That is to say, each service began covering this periodical during the year noted in the right column. Most Websites which are listed below have indicated that they will either post, disseminate, compile, archive, cite or alert their own Website users with research-based content from this work. (This list is as current as the copyright date of this publication.)

(continued)

Special Bibliographic Notes related to special journal issues (separates) and indexing/abstracting:

- indexing/abstracting services in this list will also cover material in any "separate" that is co-published simultaneously with Haworth's special thematic journal issue or DocuSerial. Indexing/abstracting usually covers material at the article/chapter level.
- monographic co-editions are intended for either non-subscribers or libraries which intend to purchase a second copy for their circulating collections.
- monographic co-editions are reported to all jobbers/wholesalers/approval plans. The source journal is listed as the "series" to assist the prevention of duplicate purchasing in the same manner utilized for books-in-series.
- to facilitate user/access services all indexing/abstracting services are encouraged to utilize the co-indexing entry note indicated at the bottom of the first page of each article/chapter/contribution.
- this is intended to assist a library user of any reference tool (whether print, electronic, online, or CD-ROM) to locate the monographic version if the library has purchased this version but not a subscription to the source journal.
- individual articles/chapters in any Haworth publication are also available through the Haworth Document Delivery Service (HDDS).

Russian and East European Books and Manuscripts in the United States

Proceedings of a Conference in Honor of the Fiftieth Anniversary of the Bakhmeteff Archive of Russian and East European History and Culture

CONTENTS

ABOUT THE EDITORS

Tanya Chebotarev, MA, MLS, received her MA in linguistics from Moscow State University and her MLS from Simmons College. She is the Curator of the Bakhmeteff Archive of Russian and East European History and Culture at Columbia University. Her articles about the Bakhmeteff Archive have been published in *Ab Imperio* and *Solanus*. She is presently preparing the first volume of a multi-volume set of Russian émigré memoirs from the Bakhmeteff Archive to be published by ROSSPEN.

Jared S. Ingersoll, MA, MS, holds advanced degrees in History, Russian and East European Studies, and Library and Information Science. He is the Librarian for Russian, East European, and Eurasian Studies at Columbia University. Mr. Ingersoll has written on libraries in imperial Russian prisons and the history of publishing in Russia.

Preface

In honor of Professor Marc Raeff
Who first introduced "Russia Abroad" to the world

This volume publishes nine papers from the international conference "Russian and East European Book and Manuscript Collections in the United States," held in New York on October 12-13, 2001. The conference commemorated the fiftieth anniversary of the Bakhmeteff Archive of Russian and East European History and Culture at Columbia University, the second largest depository of Russian émigré materials outside Russia.

The goal of the conference was to bring together international scholars to discuss the role of Russian and East European print and manuscript collection in the U.S. The conference organizers also envisioned a need to set an agenda for the development of new policies on access, dissemination of information and collection development for the twenty-first century, and to stimulate dialog across institutional, national, and disciplinary boundaries.

In addition, archival collections in the United States, some of them saved from certain destruction in the past, have become critical resources in the process of rewriting history and understanding the development of national identity that is taking place today in post-Communist Russia and the new states of Eurasia. The participants in this process draw and will continue to draw heavily on the intellectual legacy of their predecessors richly presented in the U.S. archives.

The organization of this volume reflects the topics of panels. The introduction, written by Professor Marc Raeff, summarizes the intellectual significance of the conference for the field of Slavic librarianship, historical research, and post-Cold-War scholarship.

[Haworth indexing entry note]: "Preface." Chebotarev, Tanya, and Jared S. Ingersoll. Published in *Russian and East European Books and Manuscripts in the United States: Proceedings of a Conference in Honor of the Fiftieth Anniversary of the Bakhmeteff Archive of Russian and East European History and Culture* (eds: Tanya Chebotarev and Jared S. Ingersoll) The Haworth Information Press, an imprint of The Haworth Press, Inc., 2003, pp. xi-xii. Single or multiple copies of this article are available for a fee from The Haworth Document Delivery Service [1-800-HAWORTH, 9:00 a.m. - 5:00 p.m. (EST). E-mail address: docdelivery@haworthpress.com].

xi

The conference was held at the New York Public Library and Columbia University. The sponsors of the conference were the Harriman Institute (Columbia University), the Institute on East Central Europe (Columbia University), the Bakhmeteff Archive of Russian and European History and Culture (Columbia University), and CEC International Partners, with the endorsement of the Slavic and Baltic Division of the New York Public Library.

We would like to convey our gratitude to all organizers and sponsors of the conference, especially to Mark von Hagen (Harriman Institute), John Micgiel (Institute on East Central Europe), Barbara Niemczyk (CEC International Partners), Frank Bohan (Harriman Institute), and Jean Ashton (Rare Book and Manuscript Library, Columbia University). We would also like to thank Edward Kasinec (New York Public Library) for his refreshing ideas and invaluable support at all stages of the project.

Tanya Chebotarev
Jared S. Ingersoll

Introduction

Marc Raeff

The end of World War II in Europe, May 1945, did not bring security to its population. In particular, thousands of Russian refugees and émigrés lived in fear of abduction and repatriation to the Soviet Union; and, in a new twist not seen before, this threat also affected archives and cultural objects. Unfortunately, these fears were far from groundless. It soon became known that Soviet authorities had seized the Russian Historical Archive Abroad in Prague (ex post facto, dubbed a "gift" from the Czech government), that refugees were forcibly repatriated from displaced persons camps, and that Soviet agents were kidnapping émigrés in France. Fear and insecurity mounted as the Cold War took root, culminating in the near-panic atmosphere at the outbreak of the Korean War. Russian émigrés, especially of the so-called "second wave," frantically sought refuge across the ocean; and they also looked for a safe haven for their papers, libraries, and art collections.

In this atmosphere it was natural for Russian librarians and scholars in the United States to think of providing a haven to private and institutional archives of the Russian emigration in Europe. Boris I. Nikolaevskii, having recovered part of his archival collections that had been hidden in France during the war, actively agitated for the re-creation of a Russian Archive Abroad in the United

Marc Raeff is Professor Emeritus, Columbia University, and the first Bakhmeteff Professor there.

Address correspondence to the author at: 479 Knickerbocker Road, Tenafly, NJ 07670 USA.

[Haworth co-indexing entry note]: "Introduction." Raeff, Marc. Co-published simultaneously in *Slavic & East European Information Resources* (The Haworth Information Press, an imprint of The Haworth Press, Inc.) Vol. 4, No. 4, 2003, pp. 1-3; and: *Russian and East European Books and Manuscripts in the United States: Proceedings of a Conference in Honor of the Fiftieth Anniversary of the Bakhmeteff Archive of Russian and East European History and Culture* (eds: Tanya Chebotarev and Jared S. Ingersoll) The Haworth Information Press, an imprint of The Haworth Press, Inc., 2003, pp. 1-3. Single or multiple copies of this article are available for a fee from The Haworth Document Delivery Service [1-800-HAWORTH, 9:00 a.m. - 5:00 p.m. (EST). E-mail address: docdelivery@haworthpress.com].

10.1300/J167v04n04_01

States. He found a sympathetic response from academic acquaintances like professors M. M. Karpovich, P. E. Mosely, G. V. Vernadsky, and the promise of financial support from B. A. Bakhmeteff, G. Wasson, and others. Their combined efforts led to the creation of a Russian and East European Archive which the Provost of Columbia University, Grayson Kirk, agreed to house in the University Library. The formal agreement was signed in April 1951. This was the birth of what became known, eventually, as the Bakhmeteff Archive of Russian and East European History and Culture, in recognition of Bakhmeteff's financial contribution.

The Archive developed rapidly, largely thanks to the efforts of its first curator, Lev F. Magerovsky, who had curated the collection of serials at the Russian Historical Archive Abroad in Prague. All over the world, émigré individuals and institutions were cajoled into selling or donating their papers, correspondence, and mementos to the Bakhmeteff Archive–and these efforts continue to this day. Within a decade or two it became the second largest–after the Hoover Institution–depository of Russian émigré archival materials anywhere outside the Soviet Union. After Magerovsky's retirement, his successors–Stephen Corrsin, Ellen Scaruffi, and Tanya Chebotarev–energetically pursued the development and cataloging of the Archive's holdings, acquiring, among others, important documents pertaining to East Central Europe, as well as the papers of American personalities who had played an active role in Slavic and East European events.

It is, therefore, most fitting that the fiftieth anniversary of the founding of the Bakhmeteff Archive was celebrated by a scholarly conference, held in October 2001 at Butler Library of Columbia University and the New York Public Library. The present volume testifies loudly to the success and high level of the conference. Not all of the papers presented on that occasion could be published here, but the present selection constitutes a significant contribution in the field of Slavic librarianship and historical research.

In a first group of essays we have analyses based largely on documentation in the Bakhmeteff Archive, of Russian émigré thinking on the history and future prospects of their homeland. Professor Oleg Budnitskii is the first to have seriously studied Boris Bakhmeteff's career and thought about Russia's economic and political destiny. His work goes a long way toward documenting and explaining Bakhmeteff's role in the development of Russian studies in the United States. The stimulating article by Sergei Glebov describes the main ideological components of Eurasianism, the most interesting and original political conception developed in the Russian emigration between the world wars, and which seems to have significant appeal in Russia today. For its part, the contribution by Igor Torbakov chronicles the vagaries of responses by leading émigré thinkers to the crucial fact of Russia's multi-ethnicity–a fact tragically neglected by the Russian intelligentsia before the revolution. One particular example of this neglect is the history of the immigration to the United States of the ethnic Germans from the Russian (and Soviet) empire–Mennonites and Volga Germans. In presenting an outline of this history, Professor Norman Saul highlights the interest it presents for the history of immigration to America, as well as for the ethno-social history of Russia.

The second group of papers, by Robert Davis, Jared Ingersoll, and Maciej Siekierski, considers the history and character of the formation of Slavic collections in the New York Public Library, Columbia University Library, and of the Polish archival collection at the Hoover Institution.

Last, but not least, Robert Scott and Patricia K. Grimsted call attention to some critical issues affecting the future of Slavic archives, particularly, though not exclusively, in the United States. Scott describes the opportunities and problems created by the explosive technological advances in digitizing archival documentation, enabling its ready accessibility anywhere in the world where the proper equipment is available. To the extent that I understand the technicalities of his presentation it means that a revolution in the practices and purposes of scholarship is at hand–whether for better of for worse remains to be seen.

Grimsted, drawing on the impressive experience of her long career and extraordinarily effective research, discusses the implications of Soviet and Russian efforts to claim and "repatriate" archival collections and libraries abroad, regardless of their provenance, while refusing to give up what the Soviet Union seized during and at the end of World War II. This is a grim and sad story, which further illustrates and confirms the atmosphere of distrust, insecurity, and fear noted at the beginning of these remarks. It surely validates the efforts and care to secure Russian émigré materials safely outside the Soviet Union. Let us hope that her account will serve not only as a warning, but also prove conducive to the early dissipation of a most unhealthy situation in the world of archives, libraries, and cultural objects.

Quite clearly, the papers published in this volume demonstrate the importance of the efforts made by archivists and librarians in the collecting of émigré materials. They have furthered research in and advanced our understanding of the past and cultures of all Slavic and East European peoples. The world of Slavic scholarship is indeed deeply indebted to their enthusiasm and energy. We thank them and their institutions, and offer our encouragement for their future work.

Boris Bakhmeteff's Intellectual Legacy in American and Russian Collections

Oleg Budnitskii

SUMMARY. This article is the first attempt to introduce Boris Aleksandrovich Bakhmeteff, the last Russian ambassador to the United States before the Bolsheviks' seizure of power and a many-sided Russian intellectual with a variety of interests, as a political thinker. Of particular interest to researchers are materials concerning two specific collections held at the Hoover Institution and Bakhmeteff Archive at Columbia University. *[Article copies available for a fee from The Haworth Document Delivery Service: 1-800-HAWORTH. E-mail address: <docdelivery@haworthpress.com> Website: <http://www.HaworthPress.com> © 2003 by The Haworth Press, Inc. All rights reserved.]*

KEYWORDS. Boris Bakhmeteff, Columbia University, Hoover Institution, Russian émigrés, archives, political philosophy, Vasilii Maklakov, diplomacy, democracy

Oleg Budnitskii, PhD, is Senior Research Fellow, Institute of Russian History, Russian Academy of Sciences, and Professor, Center for Jewish Studies, Institute of Asian and African Studies, Moscow State University.

Address correspondence to the author at: 32 Novorossiiskaia Street, Apt. 40, Moscow 109559, Russia (E-mail: obudnitski@yahoo.com).

Bakhmeteff's name appears in two different transliterations in this article. *Bakhmeteff* is the form he himself used in emigration; *Bakhmetev* (the Library of Congress transliteration of his name) is used for material written in Russian, following the style for this journal.–Ed.

[Haworth co-indexing entry note]: "Boris Bakhmeteff's Intellectual Legacy in American and Russian Collections." Budnitskii, Oleg. Co-published simultaneously in *Slavic & East European Information Resources* (The Haworth Information Press, an imprint of The Haworth Press, Inc.) Vol. 4, No. 4, 2003, pp. 5-12; and: *Russian and East European Books and Manuscripts in the United States: Proceedings of a Conference in Honor of the Fiftieth Anniversary of the Bakhmeteff Archive of Russian and East European History and Culture* (eds: Tanya Chebotarev and Jared S. Ingersoll) The Haworth Information Press, an imprint of The Haworth Press, Inc., 2003, pp. 5-12. Single or multiple copies of this article are available for a fee from The Haworth Document Delivery Service [1-800-HAWORTH, 9:00 a.m. - 5:00 p.m. (EST). E-mail address: docdelivery@haworthpress.com].

10.1300/J167v04n04_02

5

Private property, sovereignty of the people, democracy, decentralization, and patriotism–these are the ideas, "around which the world outlook of the future Russia is already crystallizing," wrote Boris Bakhmeteff, the Russian ambassador to Washington, DC. He supposed the basis for economy to be "private initiative, energy, and capital. The whole state and legal mechanism will adjust to patronize and protect it; the main function of the government will be helping the private initiative."[1] Bakhmeteff was an advocate of the government's "self-reduction." He relied on private initiative and enterprise: "we should set it as a rule not to compile too many laws and to regulate life the least possible."[2]

It is amazing that these ideas, which are now being widely discussed by contemporary Russian politicians, were formulated by Bakhmeteff about eighty years ago. Bakhmeteff's biography has not been written yet,[3] and his political and diplomatic activity has not been studied thoroughly enough: he remains largely unknown as a political thinker. Meanwhile, his life, deeds, and reflections are not solely of historic interest. His ideas about the future economic and political system of Russia, about its position in the world, about Russian-American relations still sound fresh and modern and can be properly evaluated in his native country only now.

Boris Aleksandrovich Bakhmeteff (1880-1951) was an engineer and a scientist, but not a professional diplomat. In Russia he not only taught in a number of universities and institutes, but also took part in the realization of several technical and construction projects. After the February Revolution, Bakhmeteff became a Deputy Minister of Industry and Trade of the Provisional Government. In April 1917, he was appointed to the position of an ambassador to Washington, DC. Bakhmeteff arrived in the United States in June of 1917 and, as it turned out, stayed forever.

In 1922, he had to abandon his diplomatic post. He established the Lion's Match Factory and later channeled much of his income through the Humanities Fund into supporting Russian émigré educational and charitable endeavors.[4] Bakhmeteff became a Professor of Engineering at Columbia University and published a number of scientific works in English on hydraulics and hydraulic engineering.[5] In 1934, he accepted American citizenship and subsequently became active in the Republican Party. In 1945, Bakhmeteff was elected chairman of an engineering foundation, which had been established largely by his efforts. Bakhmeteff was among those who initiated establishment of the Archive of Russian History and Culture at Columbia University. Shortly after his death in 1951, the archive "was included within the budget of the Columbia University Library and received a substantial portion of its operating costs from the Humanities Fund. In 1975, after the remainder of the Humanities Fund had been transferred to Columbia University, the archive was named in Bakhmeteff's honor."[6]

Despite the absence to date of a general biography, Bakhmeteff's diplomatic activity has attracted historians' attention.[7] Historians have different judgments of Bakhmeteff's diplomatic work, but all agree that his influence upon the policies of the Wilson administration was profound; for example, the sixth of Wilson's fourteen points, regarding Russia's right to determine the structure of her own government and pledging foreign assistance, was adopted after consulting the Russian ambassador. Bakhmeteff was the embodiment of the new democratic Russia for the president as well as for many representatives of his administration. However, despite the attention paid to his diplomatic activity, Bakhmeteff has remained unknown as a political thinker until recently. This can be explained by the fact that historians have not looked into his personal papers, limiting their study to the official documents that originated from his pen.

The literary legacy of Bakhmeteff remains almost completely unpublished (except for several articles and brochures he published in English in the 1920s).[8] He expressed many of his political and philosophical ideas in letters, of which he wrote hundreds during his lifetime. These bear little resemblance to typical business correspondence–many run to 20 or 30 pages and are, in essence, treatises. Along with general discourses, they contain unique information on various circumstances of his work as Ambassador and later as an unofficial representative of anti-Bolshevik Russia in the United States.

The most important of Bakhmeteff's materials are located in the United States in two places: at the Bakhmeteff Archive of Columbia University, where his personal papers are held, and at the Hoover Institution Archives (Stanford University). The Bakhmeteff Papers at the Bakhmeteff Archive consist of over eighty boxes of documents, including a most interesting correspondence, which occupies ten boxes. Among his correspondents were prominent Russian politicians and diplomats, including former Chairmen of the State Duma Aleksandr Guchkov and Mikhail Rodzianko; the leader of the Constitutional Democrats, Pavel Miliukov; chairman of the Conference of Russian Ambassadors, Mikhail Girs; Russian representatives and, in Paris, Vasilii Maklakov, and in London, Evgenii Sablin. Bakhmeteff kept up the most extensive and confidential correspondence with Vasilii Maklakov and Ekaterina Kuskova.

The Bakhmeteff Archive also contains Bakhmeteff's memoirs, which he dictated in English at the end of his life (over 600 typewritten pages).[9] However, these are less frank and interesting than the correspondence. Addressed to American readers, they contain many instances relating elementary information about Russia and Russian history.

The other important part of Bakhmeteff's literary heritage is located at the Hoover Institution Archives. The collection of the Russian Embassy in Washington, DC (474 boxes), contains a multitude of the Ambassador's notes and letters that are absent from his personal papers at Columbia University. The Girs collection is also important, for it contains memoranda and letters from Bakhmeteff including drafts of declarations he wrote on behalf of the Russian émigré community.[10] One can also find many of Bakhmeteff's original letters (hundreds of pages!) in the Vasilii Maklakov Papers[11] and some of them in the collection of the Russian Embassy in France.

Archives in Russia contain a rather insignificant portion of the texts pertaining to Bakhmeteff's intellectual heritage. Among these are originals of his letters to Miliukov[12] and Kuskova (about 400 pages),[13] which can be found in the related collections of Bakhmeteff's correspondents at the State Archive of the Russian Federation (Gosudarstvennyi arkhiv Rossiiskoi Federatsii). Documents pertaining to Bakhmeteff's diplomatic activity are located in the collection of the Russian Embassy in Washington, DC, in the Archive of Foreign Policy of the Russian Empire (Arkhiv vneshnei politiki Rossiiskoi Imperii).

In my opinion, the most interesting part of Bakhmeteff's legacy is his correspondence with Vasilii Maklakov, which continued for 33 years (1919-1951). The correspondence consists of approximately 280 letters, which amount to over 2,700 pages. It is held at the Hoover Institution Archives of Stanford University and at the Bakhmeteff Archives of Columbia University. The correspondence held at the Hoover Institution Archives is more extensive: it also contains Bakhmeteff's autograph letters, chiefly from 1945 to 1951.

It is worth noting the most remarkable fragments of this correspondence. As early as in the beginning of 1920, Bakhmeteff reached a conclusion that the main cause of the failure of the anti-Bolshevik movements was the absence of ideology that could counter Bolshevik propaganda. He considered it necessary not only to develop a program that would outline solutions of the agrarian issue, as well as the issues of nationalities and of decentralization, but also to make this program "the platform of the national-democratic revival of Russia."[14]

Bakhmeteff emphasized that the program "should not contain any concessions to Bolshevism. It must be built in its entirety upon the idea of the sovereignty of the people and the principle of private property," and include purely practical rather than abstract propositions. He considered that Russia's most pressing problem was to preserve the country's unity while considering the interests of the nationalities and local entities which comprised it. He advised not to raise the issue "of the tail and the dog" and not to become preoccupied with "who comprises whom and who recognizes whom. We need to recognize the fact from which everything else originates, that there are local rights and there is the unified Russia; the unified Russia which recognizes local formations and local rights, which in turn recognize the united Russia. The same with respect to nationalities–national entities recognize themselves to be part of the unified Russia while the unified Russia admits their entitlement to a certain complex of autonomous rights." In the future construction of Russia, according to Bakhmeteff, the principle of decentralization "should be applied on a wide basis from the very beginning."[15]

Speaking about social and economic issues, Bakhmeteff pointed out that the country's progress was tied to the strengthening and development of peasant land-ownership, on one hand, and the development of industry and trade "on the most intelligent capitalist basis," on the other. Bakhmeteff stressed that for the growth of industry it is necessary "not to get in the way, to refrain from any state interference in purely economic relations. Leave it to each and all to enrich themselves." The state must guarantee non-intervention in entrepreneurs' affairs if they observe the established laws and must "make the banker, the industrialist and the tradesman believe that his initiative and risk will not be in vain and will not be confiscated by a jealous bureaucrat at any time."[16] Now we can see that the fears Bakhmeteff expressed in January 1920 came to life in Russia of the 1990s.

Bakhmeteff also accurately determined other dangers that the new Russia would face after the fall of Bolshevism, namely, disappointment with democratic values. "A Constituent Assembly gathered on blank space will discredit itself and drown in the abyss of plain talk . . . We cannot suppose that it is possible to gather 500 or 600 people together and expect them to somewhat fruitfully compose and even discuss any programs and statements." Thus, Bakhmeteff predicted the subsequent sad destiny of the Russian Supreme Soviet. He also predicted "perestroika" 65 years before its beginning and pointed out the reason of its failure: "The crisis is in the futile use of the scraps of capitalist economy to strengthen the building of socialism."

Maklakov's apprehensions for Russia under the New Economic Policy also could have been drawn from the pages of today's papers: "There started not earnest work when the worker, the employer, and their customer all feel cohesion of their interests, but rather pure speculation and ridiculous and indecent burning of money obtained for nothing. When you see what's happening there in terms of work and trade, you inevitably fear that in a short period of time private property and capital, which so far have been the bearers of hope, will manifest themselves in such a repulsive manner that it will cause a new and, this time, a more deliberate and serious tide of hatred for capital and the bourgeoisie."

From Bakhmeteff's point of view the biggest danger for the post-Bolshevik Russia will be the great-power psychology: "The signs of Russian 'great-power,' which is exercised even by the Bolsheviks, will undoubtedly flatter a certain national self-esteem. . . . It goes without saying that along with the fall of Bolshevism the mirage of great power will turn to ashes, while the lingering of crisis can have tremendous consequences for Russia and world civilization. That's why I consider it necessary to start a merciless fight against the chauvinism, which could come to love the ghost of being a great power. All this in the language of Russian soldiery is called 'to show something to somebody' and 'punch somebody in the face' (*komu-to chto-to pokazat' i komu-to nabit' mordu*)."[17]

It is clear that Bakhmeteff was notably influenced by the American system of values and American way of life–or, more precisely, by his somewhat idealized vision of it. Denoting the new Russia as bourgeois Russia in one of his letters and its new ideology as bourgeois self-consciousness, Bakhmeteff stressed that he intended the American version of capitalism. Bakhmeteff referred to conversations with Herbert Hoover, who once told him that capitalism in Europe and in the United States were two absolutely different things, that there was no such capitalism in America as it had been described by Karl Marx, and that while the basis of European capitalism was formed by the idea of exploitation, the American one was grounded upon the idea of equal opportunities.[18]

The absence of rigid partitions within society and the possibility of "vertical" movement grants social stability. A successful person is viewed not with jealousy, but with approval: Carnegie and Rockefeller are folk heroes because they were successful. Hence, class antagonism, which gave birth to Socialism, was absent in America. According to Bakhmeteff's observations, the dominant stimulus in American society is competition. The major social stimulus is the urge to climb. Ambition is the motive force behind such upward movement. People are evaluated according to whether they possess ambition or not. The state is the property of people, it is a collective organism that preserves freedom and the equality of opportunity. Americans view their state as an establishment for preservation of freedom, and that is why the predominant attitude is not nihilism toward the state system, but loyalty, devotion, and readiness to protect the establishments that let everyone seek and receive fruits of their striving. Observations of American life brought Bakhmeteff to conclude that the possibility of a "solid political and social system is based upon real sovereignty of the people", and that "people's power does not contradict a stable conservative social system."[19]

When I first read the correspondence between Bakhmeteff and Maklakov, I was amazed by its intellectual level, literary brilliance, and even prophetical foresight of what happened to Russia subsequently. Unfortunately, their prolific philosophical and intellectual ideas have remained unknown until recently.

The study of the life and activities of Boris Bakhmeteff, this "Russian American" not only will bring a better understanding of key moments in Russian history in one of its most dramatic periods, but also will shed light on inadequately investigated aspects of Russian-American relations. Vasilii Maklakov, a friend and a colleague of Bakhmeteff, once called him a revolutionary in the sense that whereas other opponents of Bolshevism wanted to overthrow the Communist regime to revive the old Russia, Bakhmeteff's aim was the construction of a new Russia, open and democratic. The study and introduction of Bakhmeteff's intellectual legacy into scholarly and public circulation will undoubtedly promote the establishment of democratic values in a new Russia. That Russia seems eager to accept the things that the Ambassador of the non-existent government discussed, while it manages to make all the mistakes that he warned about.

NOTES

1. O.V. Budnitskii, "V poiskakh novoi Rossii" (In Search of New Russia), *Otechestvennaia istoriia* 4 (1997): 170.

2. B. A. Bakhmeteff to V. A. Maklakov, 19 January 1920, *"Sovershenno lichno i doveritel'no!" B. A. Bakhmetev-V. A. Maklakov: perepiska 1919-1951* ("Completely Personal and Confidential!" B. A. Bakhmeteff-V. A. Maklakov: Correspondence 1919-1951), ed. Oleg Budnitskii, vol. 1 (Moscow: ROSSPEN; Stanford: Hoover Institution Press, 2001), 164.

3. Basic information about him can be found in the following obituaries and articles: "Pamiati B. A. Bakhmeteva," (In Memory of B. A. Bakhmeteff) *Novyi zhurnal* 26 (1951), 252-254; N. S. Timashev, "B. A. Bakhmetev," *Vozrozhdenie* 19 (1952), 199-200; "Bakhmeteff, Boris Alexander," *Who Was Who in America*, vol. 3 (Chicago, 1960), 44; V. Borisov, "Bakhmetev, Boris Aleksandrovich," in *Russkoe zarubezh'e: zolotaia kniga emigratsii: entsiklopedicheskii slovar'* (The Russian Abroad: Golden Book of the Emigration: Encyclopedic Dictionary) (Moscow: ROSSPEN, 1997), 70-71; O. V. Budnitskii, "B. A. Bakhmetev–posol v SShA nesuschestvuiushchego pravitel'stva Rossii" (B. A. Bakhmeteff: Ambassador to the USA of the Non-Existent Government of Russia), *Novaia i noveishaia istoriia* 1 (2000): 134-166; O. V. Budnitskii, "Posly nesuschestvuiuschei strany" (Amabassadors of a Non-Existent Country), in *"Sovershenno lichno i doveritel'no!"* vol. 1, 16-114.

4. See Michael Karpovich, "Memoranda Concerning Grants by the Humanities Fund," Boris Aleksandrovich Bakhmeteff Papers, box 14, Bakhmeteff Archive of Russian and East European History and Culture, Rare Book and Manuscript Library, Columbia University.

5. *Hydraulics of Open Channels* (New York and London: McGraw-Hill, 1932); *The Mechanics of Turbulent Flow*, 2d ed. (Princeton: Princeton University Press, 1932, 1941).

6. Tanya Chebotarev, "Collections of Memoirs at the Bakhmeteff Archive," *Solanus,* New Series 15 (2001): 88-89.

7. For example, see George Kennan, *Soviet-American Relations, 1917-1920,* vol. 2, *The Decision to Intervene* (Princeton: Princeton University Press, 1989); Robert Maddox, *The Unknown War in Russia* (San Rafael, Calif.: Presidio Press, 1977); Linda Killen, *The Russian Bureau: A Case Study in Wilsonian Diplomacy* (Lexington, KY: University Press of Kentucky, 1983); David Foglesong, *America's Secret War Against Bolshevism: U.S. Intervention in the Russian Civil War, 1917-1920* (Chapel Hill and London: University of North Carolina Press, 1995); Frederick L. Schuman, *American Policy Toward Russia Since 1917: A Study of Diplomatic History International Law and Public Opinion* (New York: International Publishers, 1928), 45-49, 223-229; John M. Thompson, *Russia, Bolshevism and the Versailles Peace* (Princeton: Princeton University Press, 1966), 62-81, 280-281; R. Sh. Ganelin, *Rossiia i SShA. 1914-1917* (Leningrad: Nauka, 1969); R. Sh. Ganelin, *Sovetsko-Amerikanskie otnosheniia v kontse 1917-nachale 1918 g.* (Leningrad: Nauka, 1975), 50-53; Linda Killen, "Search for a Democratic Russia: Bakhmetev and the United States," *Diplomatic History* 2, no. 3 (Summer 1978): 237-256.

8. "Russia at the Cross-Roads," *Foreign Affairs* 2, no. 3 (March 1924): 421-435; "The NEP in Eclipse," *The Slavonic Review* 3, no. 8 (December 1924): 259-271; *The Legacy of War-Peace: A Lecture at Milton Academy on the Alumni War Memorial Foundation June 3, 1927* (Boston and New York: Houghton Mifflin, 1927); "Ten years of Bolshevism," *Foreign Affairs* 6, no. 4 (July 1928): 587-599.

9. Bakhmeteff Archive of Russian and East European History and Culture, boxes 37-38, Rare Book and Manuscript Library, Columbia University.

10. Mikhail Girs Collection, box 44, folders 2-4, Hoover Institution Archives (HIA), Stanford University, Stanford, California.

11. Vasilii Maklakov Papers, boxes 3-6, HIA.

12. P. N. Miliukov, *fond* 5856, *opis'* 1, *edinitsa khraneniia* 192b, Gosudarstvennyi arkhiv Rossiiskoi Federatsii (GARF).

13. E. D. Kuskova, *fond* 5865, *opis'* 1, *edinitsa khraneniia* 41, GARF.

14. B. A. Bakhmetev to V. A. Maklakov, 19 January 1920, in Oleg Budnitskii, ed., *"Sovershenno lichno i doveritel'no!"* 161.

15. Ibid., 161-162.

16. Ibid., 164-165.

17. Ibid., 164-165.

18. B. A. Bakhmeteff to V. A. Maklakov, 23 March 1922, Vasilii Maklakov Papers, box 4, folder 4, HIA.

19. Ibid.

Science, Culture, and Empire: Eurasianism as a Modernist Movement

Sergei Glebov

SUMMARY. The article explores the ideas of the Eurasianist movement on the unity and diversity of Eurasia, gives an overview of the role of non-Russian peoples in Russian history and culture as seen by the Eurasianists and describes the main characteristics of Eurasianist doctrine. It also discusses the semantic knot of the Eurasianist discourse, namely, the 1917 Revolution, which was accepted as the opening of a new era for Russia. In conclusion, Eurasianist views on art are introduced. *[Article copies available for a fee from The Haworth Document Delivery Service: 1-800-HAWORTH. E-mail address: <docdelivery@haworthpress.com> Website: <http://www.HaworthPress.com> © 2003 by The Haworth Press, Inc. All rights reserved.]*

KEYWORDS. Eurasianism, Russian émigrés, nationalities, political philosophy, ethnic relations, Russia, Russian Empire, Soviet Union

---

Sergei Glebov is a doctoral candidate at Rutgers University History Department and an editor of the journal *Ab Imperio*.

Address correspondence to the author at: Rutgers University, History Department, 16 Seminary Place, New Brunswick, NJ 08901 USA (E-mail: glebov@rci.rutgers.edu).

[Haworth co-indexing entry note]: "Science, Culture, and Empire: Eurasianism as a Modernist Movement." Glebov, Sergei. Co-published simultaneously in *Slavic & East European Information Resources* (The Haworth Information Press, an imprint of The Haworth Press, Inc.) Vol. 4, No. 4, 2003, pp. 13-31; and: *Russian and East European Books and Manuscripts in the United States: Proceedings of a Conference in Honor of the Fiftieth Anniversary of the Bakhmeteff Archive of Russian and East European History and Culture* (eds: Tanya Chebotarev and Jared S. Ingersoll) The Haworth Information Press, an imprint of The Haworth Press, Inc., 2003, pp. 13-31. Single or multiple copies of this article are available for a fee from The Haworth Document Delivery Service [1-800-HAWORTH, 9:00 a.m. - 5:00 p.m. (EST). E-mail address: docdelivery@haworthpress.com].

10.1300/J167v04n04_03

Eurasia is a geographical, economic and historical whole.

–Nikolai Trubetskoi

In the aftermath of World War I and the Russian Revolution, the movement of the Eurasianists was perhaps the most original intellectual product of the Russian émigré world. A reaction to the profound crisis of the old European order, Eurasianism was a peculiar combination of advanced scholarly inquiry, with implications for the emergence of the structuralist paradigm in social sciences and humanities; intense interest in modernist literature and art, with its search for a new social and cultural form; and illiberal politics similar to German and Italian fascism. The background for this combination was formed by the Russian romantic tradition and by the problem of unity or heterogeneity of the geographical, cultural, and historical space of the former Russian empire.

Eurasianism attracted very little attention from scholars during the twentieth century: most works on Eurasianism published after World War II were written by literary scholars and linguists interested in ideological motivations of the two great structuralists of the twentieth century, Roman Jakobson and Nikolai Trubetskoi, rather than by historians, with the major exceptions of Otto Böss and Nicholas V. Riasanovsky.[1] As the Soviet Union entered its last years, there appeared a renewed interest in Eurasianism.[2] Researchers have overwhelmingly considered Eurasianism within the context of the specifically Russian conservative ideological tradition of anti-Westernism, thus omitting an important aspect of the movement: its similarity with the inter-war modernist movements that intellectually paved the way for the dictatorial states in Europe.[3]

One can try to trace the elements of the alternative language of modernity functioning in the Eurasianist discourse on different levels. In philosophical pronouncements, this language implied a neo-romantic conceptualization of the Russian cultural and political space with its particularistic and anti-colonialist rhetoric; resistance to the modern bourgeois world of Europe; and an exalted proclamation of the new world. In art, the Eurasianists sought to describe a new artistic experience, which, through experimentation in form, reflects wholeness and subsumes the individual. In science, they developed the concept of structure and applied it to their explorations of Russian historical and linguistic space. Finally, in politics, the Eurasianists proclaimed themselves to be a "third way" group, bent on pursuing a politics founded on religion and corresponding to the fundamental characteristics of social life.

MODIGLIANI-ESQUE MOSAIC OF CULTURES: AGAINST COLONIALISM

One of the impulses for Eurasianist doctrine was constituted by fierce anti-Europeanism. Unlike nineteenth-century Russian conservatives–who denied that Russia should share Europe's path of development along the lines drawn by the complex of ideas that wove together a positivist worldview, democratic procedures, and free economic enterprise but still sought to find Russia's place in Europe–the Eurasianists declared Russia a civilization set apart from the "Romano-Germanic" world. Moreover, the Eurasianists saw the world constructed of separate cultures and proclaimed each of them equal to all others.

Nikolai Trubetskoi, in his proto-Eurasianist book *Europe and Mankind*, expressed dissatisfaction with the positivist tradition rooted in the Enlightenment, which established the historical superiority of European culture.[4] For Trubetskoi, the horrors of World War I were sufficient to demonstrate the barbarity of the "Romano-Germanic" world that had superseded the barbarity of non-European "savages." European culture does not represent the norm of modernity; it is the expression of the Romano-Germanic spirit. Foreseeing the intellectual developments of the second half of the twentieth century, which strove to unveil the connection between culture and imperialism, Trubetskoi argued that Europe is not the leader of progress, but a dangerous and aggressive predator, one that maintains "progressive ideas" to facilitate its own colonial domination in the world. Russia, weakened by the Revolution and the Civil War, had no choice but to become a colonial country; the task of the intelligentsia was to struggle against the ideology of progress, which facilitated the colonial conquest by Europeans.

For Trubetskoi, the experience of the war and revolution had a global implication that transcended Russian topicality. Indeed, his book was not about "Russia and Europe," as Nikolai Danilevsky entitled his famous treatise.[5] In Trubetskoi's anticolonial vision, the new era that opened after the catastrophe of Europe during World War I would witness the rise of colonial peoples only if their intellectual leaders realize the danger inherent in the acceptance of European values and beliefs by non-Europeans.

IDEOLOGY OF WHOLENESS

The doctrine of the Eurasianists was inspired by a romantic search for wholeness. In history, politics, art, or geography, they looked for concepts that would be totally inclusive; their inspiration was to create a language, "a new culture," as they called it, which was to encompass virtually all realms of the human spirit and to build on religious foundations. The genealogy of the idea of "wholeness" can be traced in the texts by Immanuel Fichte, Friedrich Schelling, Wolfgang von Baader, Aleksei Khomiakov and Ivan Kireevsky, to name but a few representatives of the philosophical romanticism that had an impact upon Russian intellectual history.[6] In certain ways this idea found expression in the texts of Fedor Dostoevsky, Nikolai Danilevsky, Vladimir Solov'ev, and Konstantin Leont'ev.[7] As Peter Gay has shown, the search for "wholeness" marked the intellectual climate of Weimar Germany as well.[8]

Thus, as far as the perception of "totalities" was concerned, Eurasianist teaching was heir to a long tradition of thought, romantic in affiliation but not necessarily conservative. Eurasianism (Petr Savitskii, in particular) developed, of course, under the immediate impact of Vladimir Vernadsky's "cosmism," which established the theory of mutual dependence between the biological and anthropological worlds with the Earth's "geosphere." (Vernadsky's son, George, became a convinced Eurasianist and produced a number of historical works from the Eurasianist point of view).[9] On the other hand, the Eurasianists were unusual followers of Petr Struve, who introduced an understanding of the importance of preserving the multinational state into the traditional Russian "State School" of history. Partly, this lineage of Eurasianism arose from contacts between Struve and Eurasianists (which were broken on account of differences in interpreting the Revolution).[10]

Nikolai Trubetskoi, for his part, was influenced by the thinkers of the Russian religious renaissance of the early twentieth century, of which his father, Sergei, and his uncle, Evgenii Trubetskoi, were well-known participants.[11] Trubetskoi might have disdained certain representatives of this generation of philosophers, (in a letter to Suvchinskii he characterized Berdiaev as "first of all a light-minded person"[12]), but he was at times intellectually closer to them than to his Eurasianist friends, since his traditional Orthodoxy precluded both pro-Soviet inclinations and excitement about modernist art.

Nevertheless, Nikolai Trubetskoi might have experienced the impact of his father's philosophical work. Sergei Trubetskoi, a professor and a liberal rector of Moscow University in 1905, continued the romantic tradition of the Slavophiles and Vladimir Solov'ev. In the elder Trubetskoi's philosophy the concept of *sobornost'*[13] played a fundamentally important role; his insistence that a human subject can be viewed as such only when it represents the whole, the society, and his critique of the West European tradition (in its positivist and empiricist or German idealist variations) were in some degree echoed by the Eurasianists.[14] Sergei Trubetskoi's ideas of "metaphysical socialism" could have inspired Trubetskoi's vision of "ideocratic" societies, while his pronouncements on the sickness of Russian literature and his critique of the "democratic" traits in it was later reinforced by Savitskii.[15]

The Eurasianists themselves admitted their Slavophile roots. As Savitskii wrote in 1922, Eurasianism belongs to one of two Russian traditions. The tradition of Aleksei Khomiakov and Ivan Kireevsky, Nikolai Gogol, Fedor Dostoevsky, Nikolai Leskov and Konstantin Leont'ev, an anti-enlightenment, romantic and neo-romantic tradition inspired Eurasianism, in adamant opposition to the tradition of the radical intelligentsia, with its positivist worldview, its veneration of science, and its religious nihilism.[16] For Petr Savitskii, this tendency was personified by Nikolai Dobroliubov, Aleksandr Pisarev, and Nikolai Mikhailovsky and the enlighteners and rulers of Soviet Russia descended from this intelligentsia tradition of criticism and nihilism.

Yet, there were important differences between the Slavophiles and the Eurasianists. Leaving aside the nineteenth-century Slavophile dream of Slavic unity, the Eurasianists believed that Russians are related ethnographically not to the Slavs of the West (Poles or Czechs), but to the Turanian world of Turkic and Mongolic nomads of the East, as illustrated by their irrational and poetic spirit, that of observers and contemplators.[17] Having observed the disintegration of the Russian Empire during the Civil War and the emergence from its ruins of national and quasi-national state units, the Eurasianists were very much concerned about the unity of Russia as a state and as a cultural region.

This concern provided the most important context for their doctrine. In their search for romantic wholeness, they stressed the positive role of non-Slavic peoples in the formation of the Russian state, declaring these peoples full-fledged participants in the organic growth of the state rather than merely passive subjects of Russian colonization. As Savitskii explained in what was the first geographical and ethnographical outline of Eurasianism, "The opposition of Russia and Europe is based, in ideological and military spheres, not only upon ethnographic Russia but on the whole range of peoples that joined her. The forces of these peoples were partly responsible for the creation of Russian power and Russian culture. . . ."[18]

Savitskii understood that he was vulnerable to criticism: does not his conception substitute one colonial domination (the Russian) for another (the Eurasianist)? He agreed that the weakest peoples of Eurasia might become subjects of Russian domination. Yet he maintained that in Eurasia all peoples with "cultural potential" have constructed their relations in a way that fundamentally differs from inter-national relations in colonial empires: "Eurasia is the realm of some kind of equality, some kind of fraternizing peoples. . . . And the Eurasian culture . . . is the common possession of all Eurasian peoples."[19] This anti-colonial approach paralleled Trubetskoi's belief that Russia, through its revolution, had inaugurated a new era, when it would itself become a colonial country and the leader of African and Asian countries. Thus, a romantically inspired search for the integrity of the Russian spiritual and geographic space was unmistakably combined with anti-colonial pronouncements and cultural relativism of a new sort.

Nevertheless, Eurasianism was based on Russian culture and tradition, and Orthodoxy held a special place. For the Eurasianists, their "postcolonial" approach meant a yearning to secure the cultural and political unity of Russia as an imperial state, "a determined defense of the Russian Empire by the Eurasians," while proclaiming a new world mission for Russia.[20] According to the Eurasianists, this state unity of Russia was created by the organic development of the Russian state and a harmonious co-existence of different peoples of Eurasia. There is little doubt that Eurasianism was inspired by the diversity of the Russian Empire and tried to suggest solutions that would prevent Russia from transforming into a multitude of independent nation-states, especially given that the latter concept was viewed by the Eurasianists as a European invention.[21] With some notable exceptions, very few representatives of non-Slavic peoples took part in the Eurasianist movement, which remained Russian-centered.[22]

In the continuing search for romantic wholeness, Russia-Eurasia emerges in Savitskii's and Trubetskoi's works geographically and economically as a closed and self-sufficient natural world comprising the forest and steppe zones.[23] Petr Savitskii insisted that Russia, which does not belong to Europe, represents a world apart, a discrete Eurasian civilization. He grounded his view in the geographical theory that the Eurasian space was determined by the systemic correspondence between landscape, flora and fauna, and climate. For Savitskii, delimiting Russia and Europe can be achieved by looking at the Russian Empire in its borders of 1914.

Eurasia, then, is a specific world, "the most continental of all geographical worlds," constituted by three great plains, the main Russian plain or the White Sea-Caucasian plain, the Siberian plain, and the Turkestan plain, which together form a single space of plains.[24] This Eurasian world, separated from both Europe and Russia, is characterized by the same type of climate, the range of temperature, and similar animal and plant life. In a remark that begets speculation about the roots of structuralist thinking, Savitskii questions whether there is a "certain parallelism" of the spiritual and the geographical spaces of Eurasia, a new third continent that he discovered in the Old World.[25]

Historically, the Russian state, having inherited the territory of the Mongol Empire, became the guarantor of Eurasian unity and realized the victory of the forest over the steppe in the internal conflict between the two. The Eurasianists took this conflict to be a source of the historical dynamic of Eurasia.[26] The impact of Mongol domination on the eastern Slavs was positive, according to the Eurasianists, since it secured the political and cultural unity of Eurasia.[27] The natural course of Eurasian history was broken by Peter the Great's reforms that destroyed the salutary wall separating Russia from Europe and that helped promote the "cultural colonization" of Russia, as the educated classes' European education and customs began to differ increasingly from the Eurasian masses of the people.[28]

Thus, the regime of imperial Russia was based on the domination by a Europeanized educated class and a Europeanized state over the aboriginal Eurasian people. Correspondingly, the Revolution of 1917 was not accidental, the kind of fateful event caused by a clique of *Jacobins*, as many émigrés understandably tended to believe, but a logical, even if catastrophic, development. In the Eurasianists' discourse, the romantic idea of "wholeness" was closely tied to the necessity to "overcome the revolution" which, in the eyes of Trubetskoi, Savitskii, and others, had unveiled the historical trouble of the Russian state, its assumed separation between the "Europeanized" and the "native" layers of the population and with Russia's multinational character. In Russia, modernity annihilated wholeness: the importation of European ideas of nationalism (false nationalism, in Trubetskoi's terms) had led to the disintegration of the Russian imperial state along ethnic and national lines.

The Eurasianists attached a special meaning of redemption and renewal, pointedly religious, to the Revolution. This became the "semantic knot" of Eurasianist discourse, a knot that tied together different aspects of culture and history. The problematic of Russian history with its "breaks" and "discontinuities" had sharpened with the Revolution. The Revolution, for the Eurasianists, was not merely the price of redemption for Russia's sin of Europeanization, it also signified a tectonic shift, an opening of a new era. In this era a new culture became possible; Russia would turn out to be the leader of the global struggle of colonized peoples against European colonizers. In art, the new epoch meant the emergence of a new cultural paradigm of form indistinguishable from the creative effort and capable of reflecting the totality of human experience. Although the Eurasianists recognized the European roots of modernism in culture, they believed that decaying Europe would not be capable of building a new culture on its own.[29] Here, Russia, with its catastrophic changes, will take the lead again. The new culture which would emerge in the world, would be based on religious values and the denial of individualism that characterized the positivist, liberal, and socialist nineteenth century.

STRUCTURALISM: A WORLD OF NEW SCIENCE

Despite the obvious and admitted roots of Eurasianism in nineteenth century romanticism, the Eurasianists produced a more sophisticated vision, a modern totality, so to speak. The romantic idea of wholeness was transformed in the works of Trubetskoi and Savitskii into a notion of typological structure, so that Russia-Eurasia becomes a system-organizing concept, using linguistics, geography, history, and ethnography, which can be integrated into a single scientific and ideological field. The meaning of Russian history emerges only when its relationship with Russian ethnography, linguistics, and geography is unveiled. Thus, the meaning of geographical factors, the systemic correspondences of climatic zones, emerges as meaningful when related to the similar correspondences of linguistic factors (for example, the spread of certain phonological characteristics). Trubetskoi himself believed that linguistics was the most scientific of all humanities and, therefore, must provide a method to all other branches of knowledge.

Roman Jakobson and Trubetskoi developed these principles in their scholarly works. Trubetskoi's "Principles of Phonology" became a classic of structural phonology. Together, Trubetskoi and Savitskii elaborated the idea of the union of languages (*Sprachbund, association linguistique*), and it became an established area of geolinguistics. Arguably, this connection between the scholarly search for new methods of knowledge, particularly in linguistics, and imperialist or nationalist ideologies was to be found in late imperial Russia. As Boris Gasparov demonstrated, one of the predecessors of structural linguistics, Baudouin de Courtenay, who was the first to give a definition to the concept of phoneme, shared a vision of language acquisition with the Russian Orthodox missionary Il'minsky, who was bent on converting Muslim Tatars to Orthodoxy.[30]

This systemic thinking, with its stress on typological rather than genealogical lineage, its synchronism instead of historicism, and its "total inclusion" of elements into a system, was characteristic not only of the Eurasianists' linguistics. Savitskii developed his concept of "place-development" (*mestorazvitie*), which united historical, economic, geographical, geological, climatic, and other aspects of a given territory's existence, an approach he termed "structural geography." Savitskii not only promoted the geopolitical interpretation of Eurasian geography, which viewed the area as defined by its exclusively continental character and the minimal role played by oceanic communications in its autarchic economy, but also explored dependencies between isobars, isotherms, and areas where particular plants and animals were endemic. In Savitskii's work, too, the concept of structure, in which elements become meaningful only in relation to other elements, was combined with furious nationalism and longing for a lost unity.

In the teaching of the Eurasianists, the idea of wholeness that had developed in nineteenth century romanticism acquired a new dimension. Using modern scholarly techniques and refusing to follow the positivist path in science, the

Eurasianists combined their conceptualization of Russian geographical and historical space with a new scholarly paradigm, in which totality became more sophisticated. The concept of structure allowed a new level of consolidation of different disciplinary findings; it also attached to Eurasianism a highly unusual aura of a conservative intellectual movement, which nevertheless had an avant-garde appreciation of novelty.

ART AND MODERNITY: THE EURASIANIST VISION

Yet the search for totality of spiritual experience and structuralism as a form of thought does not fully explain the intellectual world of Eurasianism. In romantic fashion, the Eurasianists celebrated "creative effort" and thought of themselves as demiurges of the new culture. They perceived themselves as prophets of the new; they felt that the old world in literature, politics, and art was dissolving. As Petr Suvchinskii argued, the Russian Revolution should be seen as a shift of the fundamentals of human being. "The Earth opened," he proclaimed, and the process of restoration had hardly begun. The way for this restoration relies on a combination of realism and mysticism, in the "real" religious culture. Only in such a combination can salvation and an exit from the "blocked path of modernity" be possible.[31]

Even formally, the Eurasianists used the techniques of modernist literature, printing their manifestos under exotic covers and exalted titles. Nicholas Riasanovsky noted that Russian literature of the Silver Age was one of the intellectual sources of Eurasianism, with its intense interest in, and fear of, the East.[32] Yet, it seems that the impact of the Silver Age was not limited to Eurasianism's oriental themes. The Eurasianists inherited the mood of the modernist period of Russian culture. In the modernist literature of the Silver Age they saw a prophecy of the coming catastrophe and sensed that it was akin to their own feeling, in that it distanced itself from the positivist liberal or Socialist worldview.[33]

Petr Suvchinskii reproached Sergei Prokof'ev that his music, unlike that of Stravinsky, was not modern. Modernity, according to Suvchinskii in the early 1920s, was represented first of all through form in which the demon of humanity–the demon of revolutions, cataclysms, and social dislocations–could be imprisoned. Suvchinskii also proclaimed the coming of the new age in art in the regular annual collection of articles published by the Eurasianists in 1922. He believed that on its deathbed European culture had produced a new artistic era, an aesthetic revolution, in which art had become free of humanist and anthropocentric baggage. Instead, it emerged that in formal art, in which creative effort is inseparable from form, formality ceases to be a criterion and becomes the essence of the new art. Its foundation is no longer in the individuality of the artist but in his/her ability to reflect the aesthetic power of the whole. This neo-Schellingian interpretation of art underscored the paradoxical combination of religious romanticism and idealism with exaltation of modernity.

Suvchinskii believed that modern art was the first area in which the new world had gathered enough strength to break through the limits of the old: "The goals of today's art, its triumphs and conquests, transcend art's own limits. These triumphs are the first results of the experience of the new understanding of the world."[34] In Suvchinskii's view, the dominant method of modern art is constructivist and compositionist, and successful products of art are not those that are maximally beautiful in given conditions, but those that better reflect the internal laws of composition and overcoming of space, time, and material.[35] Only the inspired will is capable of mastering the material and composing it within the form of maximal expression; to achieve this, the artistic will must be free from the reflection-centered approach to life phenomena.[36]

Suvchinskii opposed the modern art of organized material to the old epoch of "dematerialized art, descriptive images, and topical expressivity." In Suvchinskii's view, "material has ceased to be a means of revealing creative processes, it has converged with these processes into one creative form."[37] Accordingly, in modern art Suvchinskii saw a weakening of the author's "I" and the emergence of single and concrete forms of understanding of the world, "a common psychic answer to life phenomena." The acceptance of extreme formalism connected with the search for religious foundations in art signified for Suvchinskii the desire to break away from the differentiating, specifying an attitude of positivist naturalism to life.[38]

Not all Eurasianists shared this vision of modern art and this sympathy to new forms. Nikolai Trubetskoi, whose understanding of religion was bound by the limits of the Orthodox revival, debated Suvchinskii's openness with respect to futurism and other modernist movements. For Trubetskoi, futurism was an attack on beauty, and since beauty is the image of God, futurism represented the anti-religious spirit of modernity. Futurism is not a style of art; it is art's destruction. "I know what you will answer me," wrote Trubetskoi to Suvchinskii in 1922, "Futurism can still develop into both directions, and it can lead either to religious art or to the negation and destruction of art."[39] In Trubetskoi's romantic vision, futurism was connected with the destructive and fragmentizing impact of modernity. He valued futurist art when it depicted the city's industrial culture, the real world of modern Europe with all its ugliness. But he resisted attempts to see such forms of art as a new method, as a means to reveal a new vision of beauty: "futurism is . . . the enemy of beauty. That is why it is modern, for modern culture is ugly. Yes, in this culture there can be no other art. But to accept futurism as art is to agree that culture will remain such or even grow worse. This is the belief of Ehrenburg and other socialists, who made an alliance with the devil. . . . Having read Ehrenburg's book I grew convinced that the source and the cause of futurism is in . . . celebrating the machine-concrete-gas, etc., European modernity."[40] Trubetskoi thought that modern art is divided into two streams: the "passeists" (from *passé*), who are stuck in the old degenerate forms, and the "futurists," who explore novel methods but tend to celebrate the ugly, modern civilization. According to Trubetskoi, Eurasianists should side with those futurists who feel the tragedy of modern culture, which the futurist method helps to reveal.

Trubetskoi tended to perceive futurist art (and modernist art in general) as yet another sign of the destructive work of "Romano-Germanic" modernity. It was related to the socialists and the left as well as to the Jews. Here, Trubetskoi came very close to the ideas professed by the German Nazis. Warning Suvchinskii against getting too much involved with the futurists, Trubetskoi wrote: "I am writing all this to you because I am terribly afraid that you, while communicating with this entire futurist gang (*s etim futur'em*), will lose the sense of measure and will give up your romantic position. You have a leftist temptation and love to the 'last outcry' the field of art. Do not forget that leftism always leads to the devil, to Antichrist, and it is not for nothing that Yids are always with the left."[41] Trubetskoi's fierce anti-Semitism (mildly described by Jakobson as "aristocratic") did not prevent him from writing an article in 1934 that criticized German racial politics and opposed the Russian émigré Nazis.[42] Allegedly, the Gestapo's arrest and interrogation of Trubetskoi in 1938 was related to that publication.

INTELLECTUAL CONNECTIONS

Eurasianism, with its interest in Russian history and culture, appears to be a specifically Russian phenomenon, a "Russian episteme."[43] The Eurasianists themselves proclaimed that they belong to the world of Russian science, distinct from the Romano-Germanic pursuit of knowledge. At the same time, the Eurasianists promoted ideas that were strikingly similar to the views of European intellectuals of the 1920s, who were disillusioned in the liberal *Weltanschauung* of the nineteenth century. There is a clear parallel between the Eurasianist hatred of Europe and Oswald Spengler's pessimistic assessment of the Old Continent's destiny. (Although, while Spengler viewed the West as corrupted and decaying, the émigré Eurasianists treated it as a dangerous and aggressive colonizer).[44]

Similar to the German "conservative revolutionaries," the Eurasianists attempted to integrate romantic discourse's search for spiritual values hidden in the popular community with both the scientific and technological innovations of the modern age and with a new aesthetics of modernist art. Already in 1921, when the first exchange of opinions between the Eurasianists took place, in a review of Trubetskoi's neo-romantic book–in which he claimed that there was no essential difference between the culture of the Australian aborigine and the culture of Europeans–Savitskii wrote that there is a difference, if not of value, then of efficiency: it was enough to compare a boomerang to a rifle to prove that. This is why colonial peoples (Russia included) must fully use modern science and technology in their struggle against colonialist and imperialist Europe. Eurasianist publications included articles on technology, while the word *nauka* (science) played a central role in the Eurasianists self-identification. Such a remarkable combination of a romantic search for the people's spirit and interest in science and technology was characteristic of the generation of German intellectuals, whom Jeffrey Herf called "reactionary modernists."[45]

European intellectuals of non-conservative persuasion also developed certain interest in colonial peoples and in inventing supranational, continental structures. Interestingly, the Austrian aristocrat Richard von Coudenhove-Kalergi, a representative of yet another disintegrated European empire and the founder of the pan-European movement, included African colonies of European states (except England) in his project of the United States of Europe but excluded Great Britain and Russia (due to their mostly outward and non-European orientation).[46] At the threshold of World War I, the colonial conflict between Germany and France led to attempts to develop a conception of "Eurafrica."[47] However, even measured against this background, Eurasianism, with its critique of cultural forms of colonialism and its denial of Russia's Europeanness, was unique.

EURASIANISM AND THE USSR: IDEOCRATIC VISIONS

The catastrophe of the European order in the war and the disintegration of the European order in Russia led the Eurasianists to consider the nature of the Russian Revolution with respect to the future state form of Russia. They proclaimed the ambivalent character of the Revolution, insisting that it appeared to be at once a climax of the European, enlightenment-rooted development of the borrowed intellectual tradition of the Russian revolutionary intelligentsia, and a liberation of the native Eurasian forces of the people. Under the thin layer of the Bolshevik regime, which represented, according to the Eurasianists, the culmination of European enlightenment tradition, the stormy and energetic life of the people continued, liberated by the revolution. It was this life of the people that was supposed to lead to a rebirth of the Bolshevik state on truly popular foundations. Such rebirth would bring about a *coup d'etat*, and Eurasianism would then have a chance to become the ruling ideology. One need not even revamp the Soviet system, which would become the ideal form of Eurasianist government. The Eurasianists foresaw the new form of the state, where the "energetic will" and the "ruling idea" would replace procedures of democracy and administration. Such a state, in its ideocratic form, will "naturally select" the leading layer of the population. In the first approximation, such states were represented by Fascist Italy and Bolshevik Russia. Yet, the first lacked deep ideological foundations, while the second, although often pursuing correct policies due to its natural "strong will nature" (*volevaia priroda*), was unable to ground itself on the true understanding of religious life.

There is a grim joke of history in the biographies of leading Eurasianists. They intellectually supported illiberal regimes and fell victim to their unpredictable logic (apart from Suvchinskii, they were all imprisoned or killed by such regimes). Eurasianism sought contacts with the Soviet regime (as is witnessed by the organization of a meeting between the Eurasianists and the Soviet boss Piatakov, who came to Paris in 1927).[48] Yet, it seems that the logic of the Bolshevik state, which was not interested in ideological modifications of its own foundations, escaped the Eurasianists. Instead of modifying the Bolshevik regime, the Eurasianists were themselves "overtaken" by the ideas promoted by the GPU. Undoubtedly, the pro-Soviet inclinations of the Eurasianists were not accidental: they were determined by the logic of their ideas. This makes it even more important to understand the place of Eurasianism "in its own time."

In the Bolshevik regime, Eurasianists valued its efficiency and its strong will, which they opposed to the inefficiency and weakness of the Bolshevism's liberal and socialist adversaries. This strong will, according to Trubetskoi and Savitskii, allowed the communist rulers of Russia to "gather the Russian lands."[49] At the same time, Trubetskoi insisted that Lenin's government had abandoned the "civilizing mission" and was pursuing a friendly policy with respect to the non-Slavic peoples of Eurasia, a policy which he argued a "historical Russian state" would pursue.[50]

While Suvchinskii attempted to combine romantic visions of "wholeness" with the emergence of the new, compositionist art based on the supremacy of form, Trubetskoi called this binding and organizing form *ideocracy*, understanding that the coming new age would be dominated by societies united around a single powerful idea. Thus, in politics, the modernist interpretation of art was paralleled by the ideology of an illiberal state that would rule using direct forms of communication with the people and grounding itself on a scientifically based understanding of ethnography, geography, linguistics, and religion. The modernity of anti-Bolshevik Eurasianists was, in some sense, the modernity of those they wished to replace at the helm of a future Russia.

Often, the Eurasianists evaluated the performance of the Bolshevik regime in aesthetic terms. They celebrated the new type of man that emerged in the revolution and valued the will and energy displayed by the Bolsheviks. They also detected such new features in themselves, for they clearly saw the difference between their own energetic generation and the old generation of Russian intelligentsia. In particular, Savitskii characterized the new type of men who were drawn to Eurasianism: strong, energetic, and assertive. In his 1924 letter to M. N. Enden, Savitskii counterposes the personal traits of the older generation of intelligentsia–exemplified for him by the "Sophians," Orthodox philosophers, such as Sergei Bulgakov and Nikolai Berdiaev, united in the Brotherhood of St. Sophia–to those of the Europeanists. He wrote: " . . . 'They' [the Sophians–SG] sense in us a different, strong-will nature (*volevuiu prirodu*), which is distinct from 'them.' In their spiritual constitution and their social action, the Eurasianists are essentially new people, when compared to the dominant type of preceding generations; Berdiaev . . . used to acknowledge that; 'they' are 'corroded' by reflection; we (for better or for worse) are alien to the reflection that takes away force. In this respect, G. V. Florovsky, for example, belongs to 'them' rather than to 'us.' I said this about Father Sergii [Bulgakov–SG]. In a slightly different form, the same can be said about N. A. Berdiaev. However, in Anton Vladimirovich Kartashev the abovementioned nature is combined with something else . . . and makes him closer to 'us,' places him in a special position."[51]

The Eurasianist eagerness to translate their ideas into political practice had catastrophic consequences for what had emerged as a purely intellectual enterprise. The Eurasianists strove to spread their ideas among Russian émigrés and to secure a mass following. In 1922, the Eurasianists were joined by a group of young officers of the former White armies. These officers, the human material of so many political movements in inter-war Europe–right wing and left–were poorly educated, but they had the experience of World War I and the Civil War, and were full of energy. Having joined the Eurasianists, they engaged in clandestine political activities. One of these officers, Petr Arapov, established a link with the GPU-organized fake monarchist organization, the Trust.[52]

The Trust manipulated the Eurasianists from 1923 onwards. It stimulated the creation of the Eurasianist political party and organized secret trips to the USSR for Eurasianist leaders. Under the impact of the Trust, the left wing of Eurasianism, which grouped around Petr Suvchinskii and Petr Arapov, began publishing a newspaper, *Evraziia*, which even for the Eurasianists looked like Soviet propaganda, presenting its readership with a bizarre mix of Soviet

Marxism, Eurasianism, and ideas of Nikolai Fedorov's philosophy of the "common cause." The movement broke apart by the beginning of the 1930s, and only Petr Savitskii continued Eurasianist activities.

***

Eurasianism brought together people of different social origins and different professions, displaced émigrés with an experience of wars and revolutionary dislocations. They shared what Gleb Struve called a sense of "catastrophic consciousness" and a strong desire to create the foundations of a new culture. As George Florovsky put it: "The 'Euraisianist group' is neither a political party nor a sect of fanatics–according to the phraseology of our days the name that suits it the best is 'the league of Russian culture.' There is no dogmatized 'teaching of faith' that unites us; we are united solely by the homogeneity of that life force with which we perceive and live through the impressions of the contemporary time."[53]

Their vision of modernity was manifold. Yet one can discern, on different levels of the language with which they described their understanding of science, art, or politics, a desire to assert a new world of totality, a new togetherness of people. In their search for the total regeneration of culture on religious grounds, the Eurasianists did not shy away from the most radical breakthroughs in science or ideology. Trying to accommodate the problems of Russian history, the Eurasianists discovered a link between colonialism and culture, developed structuralist approaches to humanities and social sciences, envisioned a new art, and shared in the intellectual climate that prepared for the coming of the totalitarian regimes of the new century.

NOTES

1. The only monograph on Eurasianism is by Otto Böss, *Die Lehre der Eurasier: ein Beitrag zur Russischen Ideengeschichte des 20. Jahrhunderts* (Wiesbaden: Harrassowitz, 1961). For Riasanovsky's contributions on Eurasianism see Nicholas V. Riasanovsky, "Prince N. S. Trubetskoi's 'Europe and Mankind,'" *Jahrbücher für Geschichte Osteuropas* 13 (1964), 207-220; his "The Emergence Of Eurasianism," *California Slavic Studies* 4 (1967): 39-72; his "Asia Through Russian Eyes," in, *Russia and Asia: Essays on Russian Influence Upon Asian Peoples*, ed. Wayne S. Vucinich (Stanford: Hoover Institution Press, 1972), 3-29.

2. Some recent works include Ilya Vinkovetsky and Charles Schlacks, Jr., eds., *Exodus to the East: Forebodings and Events: An Affirmation of the Eurasians* (Idyllwild, Cal.: Charles Schlacks, Jr., 1996), 143-74; *O Evrazii i evraziitsakh: [bibliograficheskii ukazatel']* (Petrozavodsk: Izdatel'stvo Petrozavodskogo universiteta, 1996); Assen Ignatow, "Die Neubelebung des 'Evrazijstvo'-Mythos," *Berichte des BIOS* 15 (1992);

Sergei Polovinkin, "Evraziistvo i russkaia emigratsiia" (Eurasianism and the Russian Emigration), in Nikolai Sergeevich Trubetskoi, *Istoriia, kul'tura, iazyk* (History, Culture, Language), ed. V. M. Zhivov, intro. N. I. Tolstoi and L. N. Gumilev (Moscow: Austrian Academy of Sciences and Progress Publishers, 1995), 731-762; and David Chioni Moore, "Colonialism, Eurasianism, Orientalism: N. S. Trubetzkoy's Russian Vision," rev. of N. S. Trubetzkoy, *The Legacy of Gengiz Khan and Other Essays on Russia's Identity*, ed. Anatoly Liberman (Ann Arbor: Michigan Slavic Publications, 1991) in *Slavic and East European Journal*, 41, no. 2 (1997): 321-329. Of special interest is the recent attempt to connect Eurasianism to the problem of the emergence of structuralism in the humanities and social sciences. See Patrick Seriot, *Structure et Totalité: Les Origines Intellectuelles du Structuralisme en Europe Centrale et Orientale* (Paris: Presses Universitaires de France, 1999). Important works on the subject are Jindřich Toman, *The Magic of a Common Language: Jakobson, Mathesius, Trubetzkoy, and the Prague Linguistic Circle* (Cambridge, MA: MIT Press, 1995), esp. chaps. 9-10, and Marlène Laruelle, *L'idéologie eurasiste russe, ou Comment penser l'empire* (Paris: L'Harmattan, 1999).

3. Leonid Luks compared Eurasianism to the German "Conservative Revolution." Yet, Luks paid attention mostly to the Eurasianist distaste for democracy and fascination with the strong-willed Bolshevik regime. The intellectual connections of the Eurasianists and their modernist aesthetics did not attract his attention. See Leonid Luks. "Die Ideologie der Eurasier im Zeitgeschichtlichen Zusammenhang," *Jahrbücher für Geschichte Osteuropas* 34 (1986).

4. Nikolai Sergeevich Trubetskoi, *Evropa i chelovechestvo* (Sofiia: Russko-Bolgarskoe Knigoizdatel'stvo, 1920); Trubetskoi's book was analyzed sufficiently by Nicholas V. Riasanovsky, "Prince N. S. Trubetskoi's 'Europe and Mankind,'" *Jahrbücher fur Geschichte Osteuropas* 13 (1964): 207-220; Anatoly Liberman, afterword to N. S. Trubetzkoy, *The Legacy of Genghis Khan and Other Essays on Russia's Identity*, ed. Anatoly Liberman (Ann Arbor: Michigan Slavic Publications, 1991); review of this latter publication by David Chioni Moore, "Colonialism, Eurasianism, Orientalism: N. S. Trubetzkoy's Russian Vision," review of *The Legacy of Genghis Khan and Other Essays on Russia's Identity*, by N. S. Trubetzkoy, *Slavic and East European Journal* 41, no. 2 (1997): 321-329.

5. On Danilevsky and Eurasianism, see Stefan Wiederkehr, "Der Eurasismus als Erbe N. Ja. Danilevskijs? Bemerkungen zu einem Topos der Forschung," *Studies in East European Thought* 52 (2000), 119-150.

6. See Nicholas V. Riasanovsky, *Russia and the West in the Teaching of the Slavophiles* (Cambridge, Mass.: Harvard University Press, 1952); Andrzej Walicki, *The Slavophile Controversy: History of a Conservative Utopia in Nineteenth Century Russian Thought* (Oxford: Clarendon Press, 1975).

7. On Vladimir Solov'ev, see Greg Gaut, "Can a Christian Be a Nationalist: Vladimir Solov'ev's Critique of Nationalism," in *Slavic Review* 57, no. 1 (spring 1998).

8. Peter Gay writes of the "hunger for wholeness" among German intellectuals of the Weimar period. See Peter Gay, *Weimar Germany: The Outsider as Insider* (New York: Harper & Row, 1970), 72. Pierre Bourdieu analyzed the "ideological mood" and the "political ontology" of Weimar intellectuals and their role in creating the ideological atmosphere that made possible the Nazi takeover of power in Pierre Bourdieu, *The Political Ontology of Martin Heidegger*, trans. Peter Collier, (Cambridge, Eng.: Polity Press, 1991), 7-8.

9. See Vladimir Vernadskii, *Zhivoe veshchestvo i biosfera* (Moskva: Nauka, 1994). Vladimir Vernadsky, who also founded the Ukrainian Academy of Sciences in 1918, was closely connected with the Tavrida University in Crimea. In Vernadsky's apartment, young scholars who later joined the Eurasianist movement, gathered for discussions. See Vladimir Ivanovich Vernadskii, *Dnevniki 1917-1921: oktiabr 1917-ianvar 1920* (Diaries 1917-1921) (Kiev: Naukova dumka, 1994).

10. The Eurasianist group first consolidated around the Russko-Bolgarskoe knigoizdatel'stvo, an émigré publishing house charged with publishing the journal *Russkaia Mysl'*, edited by Struve. A. Lieven, Petr Suvchinskii and Petr Savitskii were all employees of the RBK. Trubetskoi's first book was printed there, while Florovsky published his articles in *Russkaia mysl'*.

11. On Sergei Trubetskoi, see Martha Bohachevsky-Chomiak, *Sergei N. Trubetskoi: An Intellectual Among the Intelligentsia in Prerevolutionary Russia* (Belmont, Mass.: Nordland Pub. Co., 1976).

12. N. S. Trubetskoi to P. P. Suvchinskii, 1 January 1923, Collection Pierre Souvtchinsky, uncataloged, Bibliothèque Nationale de France, Département de Musique.

13. The concept of *sobornost'* (translated often as "togetherness") was a central idea of Russian religious philosophy. It reflected both a celebration of the collective nature of human society and the fascination of philosophers with the Orthodox Church (*sobor*-cathedral).

14. Sergei N. Trubetskoi, *Sochineniia* (Works) (Moskva: Mysl', 1994), 590-595.

15. Ibid., 540-545; Sergei Trubetskoi, *Sobranie sochinenii* (Moskva: Tip. G. Lissnera i D. Sobko, 1909), vol. 3, 370-382.

16. Petr Savitskii, "Dva mira," (Two Worlds) in *Na putiakh* (Berlin: Gelikon, 1922), 11.

17. Nikolai Trubetskoi, "Verkhi i nizy russkoi kul'tury," in *Istoriia, kul'tura, iazyk*, 138.

18. P. N. Savitskii, review of *Evropa i chelovechestvo*, by Nikolai Trubetskoi, *Russkaia mysl'* 2 (1921), 134-135.

19. Ibid., 135.

20. Nicholas V. Riasanovsky, "Asia Through Russian Eyes."

21. Trubetskoi believed that copying European institutions of nationhood is harmful for the non-European peoples: Nikolai Trubetskoi, "Ob istinnom i lozhnom natsionalizme," in *Istoriia, kul'tura, iazyk*, 117.

22. One notable exception was Eren Khara-Davan, a Kalmyk scholar. An interesting, although largely forgotten, thinker was Iakov Bromberg, who developed an original version of conservative Eurasianism from a Jewish point of view.

23. On Savitskii's geographical views see Mark Bassin, "Russia Between Europe and Asia: The Ideological Construction of Geographical Space," *Slavic Review* 50, no. 1 (spring 1991): 1-17.

24. Savitskii was under the influence of V. I. Lamanskii and D. I. Mendeleev, who insisted on the geographical and cultural unity of the Russian empire. Petr Savitskii, review of *Evropa i chelovechestvo*, by Nikolai Trubetskoi, *Russkaia mysl'* 1921, no. 1-2: 130-135.

25. Ibid., 138-140.

26. The leading historian among the Eurasianists was Georgii (George) Vernadsky. Although the original Eurasianist interpretations of Russian history belonged to Trubetskoi and Savitskii, it was Vernadsky who systematized them. See his *Nachertanie russkoi istorii: s prilozheniem "Geopoliticheskikh zametok po russkoi istorii P. N. Savitskogo"*

(Tracing Russian History) (Prague: Evraziiskoe knigoizdatel'stvo, 1927). For a discussion of Vernadsky's history, see Aleksandr Antoshchenko, "Predislovie k publikatsii 'V poiskakh neevropotsentrichnogo vzgliada na proshloe': otkliki emigrantskikh istorikov na evraziiskuiu istoriu G. V. Vernadskogo," *Ab Imperio* 1 (2002), 373-386.

27. Nikolai Trubetskoi, "O Turanskom elemente v Russkoi kul'ture," in *Istoriia, kul'tura, iazyk,* 160.

28. G. Florovsky, "O patriotizme pravednom i grekhovnom," in *Na putiakh*; Nikolai Trubetskoi, "Verkhi i nizy russkoi kul'tury," in *Istoriia, kul'tura, iazyk,* 134, 140.

29. Petr Suvchinskii, "Vechnyi ustoi," in *Na putiakh.*

30. Boris Gasparov, "Eurasian Roots of Phonological Theory: Baudouin de Courtenay in Kazan," in *Kazan, Moscow, St. Petersburg: Multiple Faces of the Russian Empire,* ed. C. Evtuhov et al. (Moscow: OGI, 1997), 302-324.

31. Petr Suvchinskii, "Vechnyi ustoi," in *Na putiakh,* 112-113.

32. Nicholas V. Riasanovsky, "Asia Through Russian Eyes."

33. For a brief outline of the main characteristics of Russian modernism, see E. Lampert, *Modernism in Russia, 1893-1917,* in Malcolm Bradbury and James McFarlane, *Modernism: A Guide to European Literature* (New York: Penguin Books, 1991), 134-150.

34. Suvchinskii, "Vechnyi ustoi," 114-115.

35. Ibid.

36. Ibid.

37. Ibid.

38. Ibid.

39. N. S. Trubetskoi to P. P. Suvchinskii, 9 August 1922, Lettres de N. Troubetzkoy à Pierre Souvtschinsky, Collection Pierre Souvtschinsky, Département de Musique, Bibliothèque Nationale de France.

40. Ibid.

41. Ibid.

42. Nikolai Trubetskoi, "O rasizme" (On Racism) in *Istoriia, kul'tura, iazyk,* 454.

43. For an extended discussion of the Eurasianists' vision of "Russian science," see Patrick Seriot, *Structure et totalité: les origines intellectuelles du structuralisme en Europe Centrale et Orientale* (Paris: Presses Universitaires de France, 1999).

44. The German edition of Trubetskoi's *Evropa i chelovechestvo* was supposed to be introduced by Spengler. Trubetskoi's book was translated by Sergei Jakobson, the great linguist's brother. For some reason, the planned introduction by Spengler failed to appear in print and the introduction to the German edition was written by a well-known conservative historian, Otto Hoetzsch, who maintained contacts with the Eurasianists. There is an established connection between Spengler and Nicholas Danilevsky, one of the predecessors of Eurasianism: Robert E. MacMaster, "Danilevsky and Spengler: A New Interpretation," *The Journal of Modern History* 26, no. 2 (1954): 154-161.

45. An interesting discussion of parallels between the Eurasianists and the German "Conservative Revolutionaries" can be found in Leonid Luks, "Die Ideologie der Eurasier im zeitgeschichtlichen Zusammenhang," *Jahrbücher für Geschichte Osteuropas* 34 (1986). On conservative revolution as a modernist movement, see Jeffrey Herf, *Reactionary Modernism: Technology, Culture, and Politics in Weimar and the Third Reich* (New York: Cambridge University Press, 1984).

46. Richard Coudenhove-Kalergi, *Kommen die Vereinigten Staaten von Europa?* (Vienna, 1934).

47. See, for example, Charles-Robert Ageron, "L'idée d'Eurafrique et le débat colonial Franco-Allemand de l'entre-deux-guerres," *Revue d'Histoire Moderne et Contemporaine* 1975.

48. See "Letter to Comrade Piatakov," written by the Eurasianist Lev Karsavin on behalf of the Eurasianists, dated by 1927, Collection Pierre Souvtschinsky, Département de Musique, Bibliothèque Nationale de France.

49. Petr Savitskii, "Eshche o natsional-bol'shevizme (pis'mo P. B. Struve)," in Petr Savitskii, *Kontinent Evraziia* (Moskva: Agraf, 1997), 274-275. Yet, one has to note that Nikolai Trubetskoi strongly opposed any affiliation between the Eurasianists and the National-Bolsheviks. Actually, one can use the term "National Bolshevism" in two different ways. The first usage refers to the general trend among many émigrés to approve of the Bolshevik regime for the sake of the restoration of Russian power. The second usage, more specific, refers to a particular ideological movement led by N. V. Ustrialov. For the discussion of this movement see Mikhail Agursky, *Ideologiia natsional-bol'shevizma* (Paris: YMCA-Press, 1980); Robert C. Williams, *Russia Imagined. Art, Culture and National Identity, 1840-1995* (Peter Lang: New York, 1997) and Hilda Hardeman, *Coming to Terms with the Soviet Regime: The "Changing Signposts" Movement Among Russian Emigrés in the Early 1920s* (DeKalb: Northern Illinois University Press, 1994).

50. Nikolai Trubetskoi, "Nash otvet," in Trubetskoi, *Istoriia, kul'tura, iazyk*, 344.

51. P. N. Savitskii to M. N. Enden, 2/15 August 1924, *Fond* 5783, *Opis'* 1, *Delo* 332, Gosudarstvennyi arkhiv Rossiiskoi Federatsii (State Archive of the Russian Federation) (GARF).

52. Arapov reported his contacts with the Trust to Suvchinskii in a series of letters. See "Lettres de P. Arapov a P. Souvtschinsky (1922-1930)," Collection Pierre Souvtschinsky, Département de Musique, Bibliothèque Nationale de France.

53. Georges Florovsky, "The Letter to P. B. Struve About Eurasianism," *Russkaia mysl'* 1-2 (Sofiia, 1922): 267-274.

From the Other Shore:
Reflections of Russian Émigré Thinkers on Soviet Nationality Policies, 1920s-1930s

Igor Torbakov

SUMMARY. This paper discusses the complex ethnic situation in the late Russian Empire and the early Soviet Union as seen by Russian émigrés. Observers from many political perspectives identified that, whereas ethnic minorities often had a relatively well-developed sense of national identity within the empire/union, "Russia" was relatively undeveloped in terms of self-identification. This paradox affected both Soviet policy and émigré observers. *[Article copies available for a fee from The Haworth Document Delivery Service: 1-800-HAWORTH. E-mail address: <docdelivery@haworthpress.com> Website: <http://www.HaworthPress.com> © 2003 by The Haworth Press, Inc. All rights reserved.]*

KEYWORDS. Russian émigrés, nationalities, Russian Empire, Russia, Soviet Union, political philosophy, ethnic relations

Igor Torbakov, PhD in History, is Analyst/Consultant, Eurasianet, Open Society Institute (New York). He is currently based in Istanbul, Turkey (E-mail: igor@fulbrightweb.org).

The author wishes to thank Jared Ingersoll, Librarian for Russian, Eurasian and East European Studies, Columbia University, and Tanya Chebotarev, Curator, Bakhmeteff Archive, Columbia University, for their assistance in editing the manuscript for publication.

[Haworth co-indexing entry note]: "From the Other Shore: Reflections of Russian Émigré Thinkers on Soviet Nationality Policies, 1920s-1930s." Torbakov, Igor. Co-published simultaneously in *Slavic & East European Information Resources* (The Haworth Information Press, an imprint of The Haworth Press, Inc.) Vol. 4, No. 4, 2003, pp. 33-48; and: *Russian and East European Books and Manuscripts in the United States: Proceedings of a Conference in Honor of the Fiftieth Anniversary of the Bakhmeteff Archive of Russian and East European History and Culture* (eds: Tanya Chebotarev and Jared S. Ingersoll) The Haworth Information Press, an imprint of The Haworth Press, Inc., 2003, pp. 33-48. Single or multiple copies of this article are available for a fee from The Haworth Document Delivery Service [1-800-HAWORTH, 9:00 a.m. - 5:00 p.m. (EST). E-mail address: docdelivery@haworthpress.com].

10.1300/J167v04n04_04

The Civil War in Russia, the implosion of the imperial state and the rise of fervent nationalism among the borderland peoples of imperial Russia occasioned quite a number of discussions on the national question, especially during the empire's last two decades. Yet few observers suspected at the time how emotionally charged, explosive, and bloody the relations between nations might become. It would take the atrocities of World War I and the savagery of the Civil War to create a broad understanding that the term "nation" should be approached with utmost caution. It is highly likely that it was this new understanding that prompted Petr Bitsilli, a Russian émigré and professor at Sofia University, to pen the following lines in his 1928 essay "Nation and People": "There are ideas and notions the reckless manipulation of which can give rise not only to theoretical misconceptions but also to the greatest dangers and woes. The idea of 'nation' falls into this very category."[1]

In the eyes of the educated class in Russia, what was the most striking feature of Russia's calamitous "Time of Troubles" of 1917-1918? Probably, it was the precipitousness of the great empire's collapse. "Rus' has faded away within two days. Maximum–within three . . . It's amazing how it has all gone to pieces, to particulars," bitterly noted Vasilii Rozanov in his *Apocalypse of Our Times.*[2] "Finis Russiae," lamented the Moscow historian, Professor Iurii Vladimirovich Got'e, in the very beginning of his fascinating diary, which he started in the summer of 1917. "Former Russia has already been divided into the Caucasus, the Cossack lands, the Ukraine, an anarchist center, and, perhaps, Siberia. The Germans are proclaiming the separation of Lithuania and Courland. Russia was no longer on the edge of the abyss, but in its depths: we have passed the last barrier," he concluded.

What was the cause of Russia's national catastrophe? Got'e was convinced that "an extraordinarily ugly phenomenon" was to blame, "the absence of Russian patriotism in general and of Great-Russian patriotism in particular. [. . .] There are all kinds of patriotism in the Russian realm–Armenian, Georgian, Tatar, Ukrainian, and Belorussian–their name is legion. Only all-Russian patriotism is lacking; and the Great Russians lack it as well . . . The partial, regional patriotism that was cultivated in bygone Russia is one of the most baleful types of particularism. It has ruined many Slavic states, and it will ruin us," concluded Got'e grimly.[3]

In the celebrated collection of articles *De Profundis,* the characters of Sergei Bulgakov's famous dialogs, "At the Feast of Gods," discussed the same sad topic. One protagonist, a politician, contended that all *inorodtsy* (minorities) had national consciousness and were aggressively struggling for self-determination and autonomy. The Russians, however, had nothing–not homeland, nor patriotism, nor even a sense of self-preservation. The other character, a diplomat, responded to this with the following line: "Our people is simply not mature enough to understand [the notions of] patriotism and nationalism; it knows only its hut and its village."[4]

Georgii Fedotov–a historian, religious thinker, and brilliant political commentator–also pointed to the feebleness of Russian national feeling as a principal cause for Russia's misfortunes. In the course of the Great War, argued Fedotov, Russian people not only had run out of stamina and patience and refused to defend Russia but, more tragically, "had lost the understanding of the very idea of why Russia's existence was needed." Fedotov was truly amazed at his compatriots' attitude. In 1917, Russians "didn't feel sorry about the loss of Belorussia, Ukraine, or the Caucasus," he wrote in his famous article "Will Russia Continue to Exist?" "Let anyone who wants take it up and divide," he added with dismay. Fedotov described this kind of attitude as "we don't give a damn; we are from Riazan'," implying that Russian masses never developed anything above a vague attachment toward a concrete locality. In the wake of the 1917 Revolution, "Russian people disintegrated and dispersed into myriad peasant communities," concluded Fedotov.[5]

Thus, the majority of thoughtful observers who had lived through the upheaval of the Russian Revolution appeared to agree that the main reason underlying "historic Russia's" unraveling was the utter weakness of both Imperial and Russian national identity. Present-day scholars seem to subscribe to this view. "Tsarist Russia managed only too well in building a state and creating an empire; it failed, however, to construct a multiethnic 'Russian nation' within that empire," notes Ronald Suny.[6] In the beginning of the twentieth century, argues Ilya Prizel, "for the great majority of Russian people, overwhelmingly peasants, the Russian Empire was no more meaningful than the British Empire was to the peasantry of western Ireland . . . The bulk of the Russian people had little notion of the world beyond their village and felt no commonality with the urban intellectual elites."[7] As Roman Szporluk has perceptively put it, the Tsarist government even failed to turn peasants into Russians.[8]

It is small wonder, then, that the numerous members of Russia's "urban intellectual elites" in exile following the revolution and Civil War not only engaged in the long and heated discussions on how to deal with the national question to prevent the demise of the multi-ethnic Russian state, but, more importantly, how to approach this "accursed question" in the new post-revolutionary situation. Naturally, the Russian émigré commentators focused on two types of practice: the Wilsonian way to resolve the national question in postwar Europe, and Soviet nationality policies.

The guiding principle of Woodrow Wilson's peace declaration of 1918 revolved around the congruence of national and state borders, which appealed most to émigrés originating from the imperial borderlands. In contrast, the bulk of Russian émigré thinkers were critical of the Wilsonian model. Petr Bitsilli, for example, perceptively pointed out that realization of the Wilson program in Europe in the wake of the First World War did not result in the replacement of large multinational empires by the liberal mono-ethnic states free of national oppression. Rather, in lieu of historic empires, there emerged smaller "empires" with their own submerged minorities. The principal error of this approach, argued Bitsilli, was rooted in the mythical belief that each ethnic group (a "people") is a "potential nation" and that each people should be given appropriate conditions (its own state) under which it would evolve into a nation. "In reality," asserted Bitsilli, "the correlation between 'nation' ('culture') and 'ethnography' ('people') is different and infinitely more complex."[9]

As for the Soviet experience, the attitudes of the Russian émigré community varied widely. The representatives of the right wing simply dismissed Soviet practices as totally anti-national. Speaking at the Congress of Russia Abroad in 1926, Sergei Oldenburg stated that "To regard Soviet power as a bad, although still Russian, government means not to understand its nature." In Oldenburg's opinion, the Communists, who lacked national sentiment, were an international political sect acting on the Russian territory. The Bolsheviks, he asserted, did not reunite the country but conquered it as an external force. As he put it, they carried out "liquidation of Russia" (*uprazdnenie Rossii*). The country, noted Oldenburg with disgust, was given the outlandish name of the "USSR" and partitioned into the "states" (*shtaty*). The "cultivation of petty nationalities," Oldenburg believed, was aimed at complete ruin of the Russian national statehood.[10]

It would be more fruitful, however, to focus on émigré commentators who demonstrated better perspicacity in analyzing Soviet nationality policies, namely *smenovekhovtsy*, Eurasianists, Socialists, and some liberal observers like Georgii Fedotov.

In 1927 the émigré Menshevik publication *Sotsialisticheskii vestnik* (Socialist Herald) ran a big setting-the-stage piece by M. Verner, which opened a discussion on the national question in the USSR. Analyzing the twists and turns of Bolshevik nationality policy, Verner concluded that there did not "exist any complete Leninist teaching on the national question which could be the basis for a unified and coherent Bolshevik policy spanning the period between 1903 and 1927." In reality, he argued, the policies pursued by the Soviet Communists in the 1920s had nothing in common with what they were doing during the preceding period; Lenin himself had exercised "a practical revision of his ideas on national question," added Verner.[11]

Thus, before the revolution, being good Marxists, the Bolsheviks accorded the national question only secondary importance in the belief that national harmony could be achieved through the solution of social problems. To weaken their adversaries during the revolution and Civil War, who were fighting under the banner of "one and indivisible Russia," they actively engaged "national minorities" and launched the slogan of national self-determination. And, finally, when they emerged victorious in the Civil War, the Bolsheviks found themselves in a situation not dissimilar to that of the erstwhile imperial authorities: they had to preserve their power in the vast, ethnically heterogeneous state. At this point Lenin, who was a principled opponent of any kind of federalism, thought it expedient to establish ethno-territorial federation–to appease the borderland peoples and tie them up to the center. In Lenin's view, however, federation was only a transitional form to the complete unity of the working people of different nations.

The new Soviet federal state (or federation of states) attracted a great deal of critical attention among the émigrés. Some of them displayed remarkable shrewdness in understanding the Bolsheviks' true intentions. In 1926 Nikolai Timashev presented his analysis of the USSR's nationality policy from the legal point of view. Formally, he contended, Soviet power seemed to allow minority nationalities rights to an extent unseen before. Yet, in reality, given the strict centralization organized along the axis of party structures, "the system of fictitious national federalism" played the role of "one of the demonstrative slogans, strengthening the USSR's appeal abroad."[12] Undoubtedly, Timashev would be very much pleased had he known that both the formal structure of the Soviet Union and the very title "USSR" were indeed imposed on his Politburo colleagues by Lenin, who was thinking above all of the international revolutionary prospects. The name he initially suggested for the newly formed "federation" was even broader: The Union of Soviet Republics of Europe and Asia.

As Jeremy Smith, relying on thorough archival research, has recently shown, the contradiction between Lenin's "federalization" and Stalin's "autonomization" was not one of principle, since both leaders agreed that the Communist Party would act as the main unifying force no matter what concrete forms state relations might take. "Lenin's objections to Stalin's proposal," argues Smith, "were based on his assessment of the impact on the international revolution that the constitutional reform might have."[13] This is exactly what Timashev pointed out as early as 1926. What he could not know, of course, was the end result of Lenin's fateful decision. As Smith rightly notes, "had Lenin not insisted on the title 'Union of Soviet Socialist Republics' rather than 'Russian Federation' in the fall of 1922, the future of national relations in the region might have turned out very differently . . . The full significance of Lenin's insistence on this point could only be appreciated when the Union Republics became independent states 69 years later."[14]

Back in the mid-1920s, however, the persistent establishment by the Bolsheviks of the ethno-territorial "federation" in the country, which many had regarded as a Russian nation state, caused a great amount of perplexity within the émigré community. Discussing Soviet nationalities policy in his *Rossiia na perelome* (Russia at the Turning Point), Pavel Miliukov noted with a dose of incredulity: "They have unearthed from history and resurrected a whole number of ancient nationalities and forged out of them 'autonomous regions' and 'republics.' As a result, the map of administrative division of Russia proper now very much resembles a historico-ethnographic map of ancient Russia."[15]

These Bolshevik practices, together with the hindsight knowledge of how the USSR's history ended, have allowed some contemporary scholars to come to a somewhat extravagant conclusion. Yuri Slezkine, for instance, asserts that Soviet nationalities policy was shaped and carried out "by the nationalists." In his informative article "The USSR as a Communal Apartment," Slezkine points out that the Soviet Union was the first country to institutionalize ethno-territorial federalism, classify all citizens according to their ethnic origin, and formalize favored attitudes to certain categories of ethnically defined population. All this, he states, is evidence of the "chronic ethnophilia of the Soviet regime." As for the population of the USSR itself (the so-called "Soviet people"), they–from the formal point of view–did not constitute a *nation*–the communal apartment was not larger than the sum total of its rooms, remarks Slezkine. Despite the fact that at least since March 1925, all Soviet citizens were preoccupied with "building socialism in one country"–the one with clearly defined borders and highly centralized both politically and economically–the Soviet Union, continues Slezkine, had neither national identity nor official language and national culture. This state formation had only "socialist content," completely devoid of "national form."[16] Terry Martin resorts to less risky appellations, although he, too, terms the Bolshevik nation-builders "internationalist nationalists, or better yet, affirmative action nationalists."[17]

Valerii Tishkov holds similar views. "It would seem that the principle of 'national statehood' organized at the level of ethno-territorial autonomies for minorities took hold in the USSR as a polemical antithesis to 'bourgeois federalism' based on territorial principle." "Thus," argues Tishkov, "the metaphor of *nation* and the term *nationality* . . . were passed on to the culturally related groups of the country's population, and the task of 'nation-building' was included into the ideological arsenal of the ethnically defined intra-state formations (Union and autonomous republics, and autonomous regions)."[18]

This way of reasoning is nicely summed up in a passage by Rogers Brubaker: "Herein lies the distinctiveness of the Soviet nationality regime–in its unprecedented displacement of nationhood and nationality, as organizing principles of the social and political order, from the state-wide to sub-state level. No other state has gone so far in sponsoring, codifying, institutionalizing, even (in some cases) inventing nationhood and nationality on the sub-state level, while at the same time doing nothing to institutionalize them on the level of the state as a whole."[19]

In so doing, this contemporary school of thought insists that the Soviet state paved the way to its own demise. Self-determination and independence were designed to be empty forms, legal fictions, a game of sorts. "The longer it went on, the more literally it was interpreted [in the borderlands], leading to a series of conflicts in the party and interfering with economic policy."[20] These unintended consequences of establishing dangerous "legal fictions" were clearly identified by some émigré thinkers. Nikolai Alekseev, the Eurasianist and legal scholar, perceptively wrote that ethno-territorial federation coupled with the principle of self-determination, having gained wide currency, aroused "nationalist ghosts" inimical to the Soviet state and internationalism. The Bolsheviks, noted Alekseev, created "numerous national republics for peoples who never bothered to even think of any autonomy in the past." "It would seem," he continues, "that communist policy goes out of its way to make possible what now seems unthinkable–namely, the ruin of both Russia and internationalism by the individual peoples currently contained within Russia."[21]

Similar apprehension was voiced by Georgii Fedotov in 1929. "No one," he wrote, "will deny the dangerous significance of [national] separatisms tearing up Russia's body. Over the eleven years of revolution dozens of national consciousnesses have emerged and strengthened in its enfeebled body. Some of them already represent a menacing force. Each small people (*narodets*), semi-barbarous only yesterday, produces its own cadres of semi-intelligentsia, which are already driving their Russian teachers away." More significant, he adds, "under the veneer of international communism, and within the communist party itself, cadres of nationalists are forming which strive to break the historic body of Russia into pieces."[22]

It would be naive to believe that the Soviet communist elites, particularly Stalin, were unaware of legal and institutional contradictions built into the Soviet Union's state system. Although Stalin was the head of *Narkomnats* (People's Committee on Nationalities), he was by no means an "ethnonationalist" in Slezkine's terms. Stalin's letter to Lenin of 22 September 1922, a response to Lenin's request for information on how the issue of relations between the Soviet republics was being solved, sheds light on future Soviet policies on the national question. It also shows that, contrary to Smith's assertion, Stalin did have a certain plan in this sphere–namely, to curtail maximally the rights that the Soviet republics had gained during the Civil War:

We have come to such a position, where the existing order of relations between the center and the borderlands, that is, the absence of any order and complete chaos, has become intolerable. When the situation produces conflicts, insults and irritation, it turns into a fiction, the so-called united federative people's economy, and hampers and paralyzes all economic affairs on a Russia-wide scale. There are two options: *either* real independence, and, in this case, noninterference of the center, their own People's Commissariats for Foreign Affairs, their own external trade, their own concessions committees, their own railways; along with which, general questions are decided in the course of negotiations between equals, by agreement, but the decisions of the VTsIK, SNK and STO of the RSFSR are not obligatory for the independent republics; or *else*, the real unification of the Soviet republics into one economic whole with the formal extension of the powers of the SNK, STO and VtsIK of the RSFSR over the SNK, VtsIK and the economic councils of the independent republics, i.e., a change from fictitious independence to real internal autonomy of the republics in the areas of language, culture, justice, internal affairs, agriculture, etc.

Then Stalin makes a brief excursion into the recent past to explain how and why the current–in his view, abnormal–situation was shaped:

During four years of civil war when, given the foreign intervention, *we were obliged to demonstrate Moscow's liberalism on the national question*, we managed to nourish, against our will, a group of real and persistent social-independents (*sotsial-nezavisimtsy*) among Communists, who demand genuine independence in every sense and who rate the interference of the Central Committee of the Russian Communist Party as deception and hypocrisy on the part of Moscow . . . If we do not now strive to reconcile the form of relationship between the center and the borderlands to *the actual relationships, on the strength of which the borderlands ought in every respect to be subordinate to the center,* that is, if we do not now change formal (fictitious) independence for formal (and real) autonomy, then after a year it will be incomparably harder to achieve the factual unity of the Soviet republics.[23]

From this point of view, Stalin was perfectly right. His ideal was a centralized state, not an "institutionalized multinationality." The so-called "Georgian affair" and "Sultan-Galiev affair"[24] demonstrated to the Moscow central power that time was running out. "For Stalin and his supporters," writes Bulat Sultanbekov, "it had become crystal clear that there was a need to terminate even a limited pluralism of opinion on the national question. The time for other solutions had arrived."[25]

Some scholars of the history of revolutions point out that any radical movement, even those guided by internationalist ideology, turns to nationalism and xenophobia when it gains the levers of power: "the revolution is absorbed by the state which had earlier engendered this same revolution."[26] There exist a considerable number of works analyzing national-patriotic proclivities of Russian Marxism. However, it is always the concrete historic circumstances that amplified national sentiment inherent in Russian Communism. The first powerful upsurges of National Bolshevism occurred at the time of the Brest-Litovsk peace treaty in 1918, and then again during the war with "White Poland" in 1920-1921. Contrary to initial expectations that it would turn into a detonator of world revolution, the Polish campaign took on a pronounced national form. The *Smenovekhovtsy*, National Bolsheviks par excellence who professed an ideological mix of revolutionary patriotism, traditional Russian nationalism and renewed *etatism*, advanced a fairly accurate assessment of the ethno-political evolution of post-revolutionary Soviet society. (To be sure, they were mistaken as to the possible role the political forces of "old Russia" might play in the process.) The *Smenovekhovtsy* greeted the fourth anniversary of October Revolution as the holiday of Russian national independence. Needless to say, they enthusiastically supported Russification and centralization.

Already in March 1920 Nikolai Ustrialov, one of the National Bolshevik leaders, wrote in the newspaper *Novosti zhizni:* "Paradoxical though it may seem, the unification of Russia is proceeding under the banner of Bolshevism, which has become imperialist and centralist to a greater extent even than Pavel Nikolaevich Miliukov himself."[27] Soon, the editorial in the first issue of *Smena vekh* proclaimed the authentic Russian character of both the "Russian Revolution" and Bolshevism. Musing on the "national mystique" and "Russia's mission," the editor eventually came to a very clear political conclusion: "The examples of Armenia, Georgia, and Azerbaijan, showed where the 'national dreams of small peoples' who are historically unprepared to lead an independent existence might take them to . . . The Balkanization of Europe, too, is also not such an inspiring example to serve as a model for the Balkanization of Russia through the implementation of the principle of self-determination of peoples."[28] In the next issue of the journal S. Lukianov wrote in his article titled "Revolutionary Creativity of Culture": "The main historical and cultural task of the 1917 Revolution was to create conditions for the re-establishment of Russian cultural unity."[29]

Arguably, during the first years of the Soviet regime Stalin, while promoting centralization, was more keen to streamline the management of the state apparatus, and paid less attention to the forging of "cultural unity." However, as time went on and the international situation changed, he became more inter-ested in shaping some sort of Soviet identity. The world economic crisis of 1929-1933 did not bring about social explosions in the "citadels of capital-ism." The cherished hopes for the victories of proletarian revolutions in other countries, either in the West or the East, were dashed. The theory of "perma-nent revolution" seemed outdated and out of place. Also, the Nazis' rise to power in Germany in 1933 made the danger of war quite real.[30] Under these circumstances the regime was in dire need of loyal and patriotic citizens who, in the moment of danger, would strongly identify first and foremost with the Soviet state and not with just one individual republic. This state need caused a massive overhaul of the communist propaganda machine.

Elsewhere, I have analyzed in detail how this "great turn" affected Soviet historical scholarship.[31] Here, it will suffice to say that from the beginning of the 1930s all humanities and the way they were being taught were drastically revamped. From then on, the *agitprop*'s main goal was to fashion and cultivate all-Soviet values. Vladimir Mayakovsky, the author of the famous "Poem on the Soviet Passport" artistically reflected this new ideological trend in the fol-lowing lines: "The most important in us is our Country of Soviets, Soviet free-dom, Soviet flag, Soviet sun."[32] Then, the great leader himself stated from the rostrum of the Seventeenth Congress of the Communist party, "We orient our-selves only and exclusively on the USSR." It is not fortuitous that it was at this congress that Stalin noted with satisfaction: "[All] the nationalist-deviationist groupings have been defeated and dispersed."[33]

True, starting from the 1930s, the ideology of Soviet patriotism was being persistently imposed from above.[34] Yet it was not just a one-way process. The Soviet patriotic feeling was also steadily growing from below, and the unbi-ased émigré observers could not fail to notice this. The people, argued some liberal-minded émigré thinkers, had rediscovered "their own" Russia in the process of revolution when they got rid of the nobility and imperial bureau-cracy. Those classes had sustained the existence of the Empire but at the same time acted as a kind of barrier between the state and the people. "For the millions of peasants and workers," wrote Fedotov in 1936 in Alexander Kerenskii's periodical *Novaia Rossia*, "revolution became . . . the center of crystallization of the new elementary patriotic sentiment. Russia, liberated from the bourgeoisie, the *muzhiks'* Russia came to be perceived as their own [country]." Thus, concluded Fedotov, "the new Soviet patriotism is a fact that is senseless to refute."[35]

But what kind of state was the Soviet Union in the mid-1930s, right after the completion of the Stalin's brutal "revolution from above"? Did it become a true Russian nation state or did it evolve into a veritable empire, multi-cultural and tolerant, but with the clear-cut supranational imperial identity? On this question, the opinions of the émigré community varied. Some, like Nikolai Berdiaev, tended to view late Stalinist ideology as derivative of traditional Russian nationalism: "Communism in the period of Stalinism can be perceived, and not without reason, as the continuation of Peter the Great's deeds . . . There emerges in Russia not only communist but also Soviet patriotism which is, in fact, a pure Russian nationalism," added the exiled philosopher.[36]

To be sure, scholars today see the Soviet ideological situation of the 1930s as much more nuanced. David Brandenberger, for instance, correctly notes that "Soviet ideology's assumption of an increasingly Russocentric, etatist posture during the mid- to late 1930s took place without ever fully breaking with the previous two decades of militant proletarian internationalism."[37] Brandenberger calls the Stalinist leadership's maneuvering an "awkward balancing act." It must be mentioned, however, that some Russian émigré thinkers understood the nature of what present-day scholarship calls an "awkward ideological dualism" in no less clear terms.

Georgii Fedotov is a case in point here. Stalinist national ideology, he writes in the article titled "What Are Stalin's Views on Russian History?" was extremely contradictory. This ideology, Fedotov argued, was aspiring "to combine Marx with Aleksandr Nevskii, Stalin with Peter the Great."[38] Fedotov aptly labeled this eclectic ideological construct as "October nationalism."[39] In terms of national relations in the USSR, "October nationalism" undoubtedly meant placing stronger emphasis on Russian "traditional values" and Russian national history, but at the same time preserving all those ambiguities flowing out of the specific Soviet ethno-territorial arrangement and its accompanying ideological legitimation that was not changed. Obviously, in the 1930s and later Stalin was maneuvering; yet, he hesitated to make a decisive step.

What were his options? "Soviet elites," writes Brubaker, "might have sought to organize the same territories and peoples as a nation-state—whether as a Soviet nation state, founded on the emergent Soviet nation, or as a Russian nation state. But they did neither."[40] Among Russian émigrés, various factions were actually suggesting exactly these two solutions. The National Bolshevik Ustrialov believed that, having a powerful state at their disposal, the Communists could easily forge a new Soviet nation. "The state," wrote he, "is a primary nationalizing factor, especially a 'total,' ideocratic state." In 1933 in his article titled "On the Soviet Nation," he asserted that the population of the Soviet state is being merged into a new nation "consisting of polychrome, polyglot, multi-faced [human] material welded by one state and the power of the leading idea."[41] On the other hand, the representatives of the émigrés' right wing would only be delighted to see the Bolsheviks achieving what even the Romanov Empire failed to do, namely turning a *Natsionalitätenstaat* into a Russian nation state.

There was also, true to Russian tradition, a "third way," more democratic and decentralized, proposed by the Eurasianists. It would resemble a classic imperial arrangement with a clear-cut supra-national identity–"Eurasian nationalism," or rather a hierarchy of identities. The left-wing Eurasianist (and future Communist) Prince Dmitrii Sviatopolk-Mirskii praised Eurasianism because, "despite inherent nationalist temptation, from its very outset it showed the way toward overcoming Russian nationalism [and] underscored the supra-national character of its task by its very name," wrote Mirskii in the first article of his thirteen-part series titled "Nationalities of the USSR."[42] Eurasianists viewed Russia-Eurasia as a single geocultural entity, and the Eurasian state as a "symposium of nationalities" or "symposium of religions." "Eurasianists understand Russia as the 'symposium of peoples' (*sobor narodov*). They believe that political unity of this vast territory is a result not only of the efforts of just Russian people but of many peoples of Eurasia," wrote the leading member of the school Petr Savitskii.[43] The concept of "Eurasian nationalism" was thoroughly elaborated by Prince Nikolai Trubetskoi. Its main thesis is as follows: "The nationalism of each people of Eurasia should be combined with Eurasia-wide nationalism . . . Every citizen of such a state should realize that not only he belongs to a particular people . . . but also that this people belongs to the Eurasian nation. A citizen should take pride in both of these identities."[44]

It would appear that the Eurasianist approach toward nationality policies, in particular Trubetskoi's ideal of a voluntary union of Russia's various peoples, was not only more "liberal" than the other two options but more feasible too. Already by the end of the nineteenth century the most perceptive Russian observers came to understand that the Russian Empire simply could not carry out the nationalizing policies pursued at the time by the major European states. Turning itself into a Russian nation state was physically beyond its reach. "More than half of our population are not Great Russians. Russia is not an [ordinary] state but a whole world, bringing together [various] countries, peoples, languages, and religions," argued Vasilii Rozanov as early as 1898 in his journalistic dispatch from the North Caucasus to the influential St.-Petersburg daily *Novoe vremia*. That is why, continued Rozanov, "the objectives of Russia's existence and history differ from those of Warsaw, Vienna, or Berlin . . ."[45]

Needless to say, after the unprecedented upsurge of national consciousness in the former imperial borderlands caused by World War I and the Revolution, the task of forging a nation state on the territories of the Russian Empire became absolutely impractical. "The present-day Russian Empire has and will continue to have the form of a federation of free peoples. Otherwise, it will not be able to exist," contended Georgii Fedotov in January 1939.[46] Earlier, in 1931, in his own journal *Novyi grad,* Fedotov mused on what could potentially be a "Russian lesson" in the sphere of nationality policies: "Russia is the only extant *Nationalitätenstaat,*" he writes in the programmatic article "The Twilight of the Fatherland." "It is thus faced with the great task of the experimental building of the political cohabitation of peoples. If Russia succeeds in resolving its nationality problem, its experience could be used worldwide," argued Fedotov.[47]

Most liberal-minded Russian émigré intellectuals, however, were not overly optimistic about the Bolsheviks' ability to shape a new national identity for the citizens of the USSR. The very foundations of Stalinist nationalities policy, they believed, were too contradictory and shaky. In 1937, in the brilliant essay titled "Aleksandr Nevskii and Karl Marx," the same Georgii Fedotov produced one of the best analyses of the tangled problem the Soviet Bolsheviks were faced with:

> Official Russia undoubtedly seeks to shape its national consciousness. There is no doubt, however, that it is unable to achieve this. How is it possible to piece together the scraps of old Marxism, materialism of the 1860s and nationalism of the new [Soviet] statists? What about the need to fully absorb [the moral principles] of great Russian literature? It is obvious that the synthesis Stalin is dreaming about is unrealizable. Or, more precisely, it may be realized by way of the total shift of all values. But for this, the [Soviet] autocrat will lack both courage and, probably, imagination.[48]

Fedotov was absolutely right. The Soviet leadership had indeed come up with an ambiguous arrangement, lacking either a clear-cut imperial or Russian national identity. Besides, the ruling Moscow Bolsheviks' obsession with centralization prevented the nation-like republics that they themselves so industriously created to evolve into full-blooded political nations. In a way, this arrangement resembled the Romanov Empire in its last decades. It is possible to say that both Tsarist Russia's and the Soviet Union's experience under Stalin "was one of incomplete nation-making."[49]

This seemingly improbable continuity has, after all, only demonstrated the strength and perseverance of historical forces. As Francois Guizot once said, "When nations have lived gloriously for a long time, they are unable to break with their past, whatever they do . . . Even the most daring and powerful revolution cannot abolish national traditions which have existed for a long time."[50]

NOTES

1. Petr Bitsilli, "Natsiia i narod" (Nation and People), in P.M. Bitsilli, *Izbrannye trudy po filologii* (Selected Works on Philology) (Moskva: Nasledie, 1996), 66.

2. Vasilii Rozanov, *O sebe i zhizni svoei* (On Myself and My Life) (Moskva: Moskovskii rabochii, 1990), 579.

3. Iurii Vladimirovich Got'e, *Time of Troubles: The Diary of Iurii Vladimirovich Got'e*, transl., ed., and intro. by Terence Emmons (Princeton: Princeton University Press, 1988), 27, 78, 36.

4. Sergei Bulgakov, "Na piru bogov" (At the Feast of Gods) in *Iz glubiny: Sbornik statei o russkoi revoliutsii* (From the Depths: Collection of Articles on the Russian Revolution) (Moskva: Izdatel'stvo Moskovskogo universiteta, 1990), 113.

5. G. P. Fedotov, *Polnoe sobranie statei v shesti tomakh* (Complete Works in Six Volumes), vol. 1, *Litso Rossii: Stat'i 1918-1930* (The Face of Russia: Articles 1918-1930) (Paris: YMCA-Press, 1988), 283, 284.

6. Ronald Grigor Suny, "The Empire Strikes Out: Imperial Russia, 'National' Identity, and Theories of Empire," in Ronald Suny and Terry Martin, eds., *A State of Nations: Empire and Nation-Making in the Age of Lenin and Stalin* (Oxford: Oxford University Press, 2001), 56.

7. Ilya Prizel, *National Identity and Foreign Policy: Nationalism and Leadership in Poland, Russia, and Ukraine* (Cambridge: Cambridge University Press, 1998), 178.

8. Roman Szporluk, "Padinnia tsarysts'koi imperii ta SRSR: rossiis'ke pytannia i nadmirne rozshyrennia imperii" (The Fall of the Tsarist Empire and the USSR: The Russian Question and the Over-Expansion of the Empire), *Dukh i Litera* (Kyiv), 1997, no.1-2: 113.

9. Bitsilli, "Natsiia i narod," 75.

10. Sergei Oldenburg, "Sushchestvo kommunisticheskoi vlasti" (The Nature of Communist Power), *Vozrozhdenie* (Paris), 6 April 1926, 4, quoted in: D. N. Nikitin, "Natsional'nye problemy v SSSR v literature russkogo zarubezh'ia, 1920-1930-e gody" (National Problems in the USSR in Russian Émigré Literature, 1920s-1930s), *Vestnik Moskovskogo universiteta*, 8th ser., *Istoriia*, 1996, no. 4: 4.

11. M. Verner, "Natsional'naia problema Sovetskogo Soiuza" (The National Problem of the Soviet Union) *Sotsialisticheskii vestnik* (Berlin), no. 21-22 (1927): 13.

12. N. S. Timashev, "Problema natsional'nogo prava v Sovetskoi Rossii" (The Problem of National Right in Soviet Russia), *Sovremennye zapiski* (Paris), no. 29 (1926): 396.

13. Jeremy Smith, *The Bolsheviks and the National Question, 1917-1923* (New York: St. Martin's Press, 1999), 189.

14. Smith, *The Bolsheviks and the National Question*, 188, 240.

15. P. N. Miliukov, *Rossiia na perelome: bol'shevistskii period russkoi revoliutsii* (Russia at the Turning Point: The Bolshevik Period of the Russian Revolution) (Paris, 1927), 1: 421.

16. Yuri Slezkine, "The USSR as a Communal Apartment, or How a Socialist State Promoted Ethnic Particularism," *Slavic Review*, 53, no. 2 (spring 1994): 414-452.

17. Terry Martin, *The Affirmative Action Empire: Nations and Nationalism in the Soviet Union, 1923-1939* (Ithaca, N.Y.: Cornell University Press, 2001).

18. V. A. Tishkov, "Zabyt' o natsii: postnatsionalisticheskoe ponimanie natsionalizma" (To Forget About the Nation: The Post-Nationalist Understanding of Nationalism), *Etnograficheskoe obozrenie* 5 (1998), 17.

19. Rogers Brubaker, *Nationalism Reframed: Nationhood and the National Question in the New Europe* (Cambridge: Cambridge University Press, 1996), 29.

20. Smith, *The Bolsheviks and the National Question,* 184.

21. N. N. Alekseev, *Russkii narod i gosudarstvo* (The Russian People and State) (Moskva: Agraf, 1998), 368.

22. Fedotov, *Polnoe sobranie statei,* 1: 281.

23. *Izvestiia TsK KPSS,* 1989, no. 9: 198-199 (emphasis added).

24. The "Georgian affair" (1921-1922) and the "Sultan-Galiev affair" (1923) were the first attempts by the Bolshevik central leadership at suppressing what was called by Moscow the "national-bolshevism"–a movement within Georgian and Bashkir communist organizations that resisted the super-centralization promoted by the Kremlin.

25. Bulat Sultanbekov, introduction to *Tainy natsional'noi politiki TsK RKP* (Secrets of National Politics of the Central Committee of the Russian Communist Party), (Moskva, 1992), 9.

26. Gennadii Bordiugov and Vladimir Bukharaev, "Natsional'naia istoricheskaia mysl' v usloviiakh sovetskogo vremeni" (National Historical Thought in the Circumstances of Soviet Times), in *Natsional'nye istorii v sovetskom i postsovetskikh gosudarstvakh* (National Histories in Soviet and Post-Soviet States) (Moskva: AIRO-XX, n.d.), 28.

27. N. V. Ustrialov, *V bor'be za Rossiu* (In the Fight for Russia) (Kharbin, 1920), 5, quoted in Tamash Kraus, *Sovetskii termidor: dukhovnye predposylki stalinskogo perevorota, 1917-1928* (Soviet Thermidor: The Spiritual Pre-Conditions for the Stalinist Coup, 1917-1928) (Budapest: Vengerskii institut rusistiki, 1997), 87.

28. *Smena vekh* 1 (1921): 18, quoted in Kraus, *Sovetskii termidor,* 89. (LC transliteration of old-orthography title is *Smiena viekh.*–Ed. [KR].)

29. *Smena vekh* 2 (1921): 8, quoted in Kraus, *Sovetskii termidor,* 90.

30. See Gennadii Bordiougov, "War and Peace: Stalin's Regime and Russian Nationalism," *History Today* 45 (1995).

31. See Igor Torbakov, "Oskolki razbitogo vdrebezgi: istoricheskoe porazhenie imperskogo proekta" (Splinters of Something Broken to Smithereens: The Historical Defeat of the Imperial Project) *Ab Imperio* 4 (winter 2001).

32. V. V. Mayakovsky, *Polnoe sobranie sochinenii* (Complete Collected Works) (Moskva, 1958), 10: 119. A bit later, an analogous sentiment was expressed by another poet, the Ukrainian Pavlo Tychyna, in his poem "The Feeling of One Family," which was published in *Pravda.*

33. *XVII s"ezd VKP (b), 26 ianvaria-10 fevralia 1934 goda: stenograficheskii otchet* (Seventeenth Meeting of the All-Union Communist Party [Bolsheviks], 26 January-10 February 1934: Stenographic Report) (Moskva, 1934), 28.

34. See D. L. Brandenberger and A. M. Dubrovsky, " 'The People Need a Tsar': The Emergence of National Bolshevism as Stalinist Ideology, 1931-1941," *Europe-Asia Studies* 50, no. 5 (1998), 873-892.

35. Fedotov, *Polnoe sobranie statei,* vol. 4, *Zashchita Rossii: Stat'i 1936-1940 iz "Novoi Rossii"* (Defense of Russia: Articles 1936-1940, from *Novaia Rossiia*) (Paris: YMCA-Press, 1982), 13-14.

36. N. A. Berdiaev, *Istoki i smysl russkogo kommunizma* (Sources and the Meaning of Russian Communism) (Moskva, 1990), 120.

37. David Brandenberger, " '. . .It Is Imperative to Advance Russian Nationalism as the First Priority': Debates Within the Stalinist Ideological Establishment, 1941-1945," in Ronald Suny and Terry Martin, eds., *A State of Nations,* 276.

38. Fedotov, *Polnoe sobranie statei*, vol. 4: 135-136.

39. Fedotov, *Polnoe sobranie statei*, vol. 3, *Tiazhba o Rossii: Stat'i 1933-1936* (Competition for Russia: Articles 1933-1936) (Paris: YMCA-Press, 1982), 289.

40. Brubaker, *Nationalism Reframed*, 28.

41. N. V. Ustrialov, *Nashe vremia* (Our Time) (Shanghai, [1934?]), 35.

42. Dmitrii Sviatopolk-Mirskii, "Natsional'nosti SSSR" (Nationalities of the USSR), *Evraziia* (Paris) 22 (1929).

43. Petr Savitskii, *Kontinent Evraziia* (The Continent of Eurasia) (Moskva: Agraf, 1997), 110.

44. N. S. Trubetskoi, *Istoriia, kul'tura, iazyk* (History, Culture, Language) (Moskva, 1995), 424.

45. Vasilii Rozanov, *Inaia zemlia, inoe nebo . . . Polnoe sobranie putevykh ocherkov 1899-1913 gg.* (Another World, Another Sky: Complete Collected Travel Sketches, 1899-1913) (Moskva: Tanais, 1994), 17.

46. Fedotov, *Polnoe sobranie statei*, 4: 220.

47. Fedotov, *Polnoe sobranie statei*, 2: 154.

48. Fedotov, *Polnoe sobranie statei*, 4: 92-93.

49. Suny, "The Empire Strikes Out," 56.

50. Quoted in Hans Kohn, "Soviet Communism and Nationalism: Three Stages of a Historical Development," in *Soviet Nationality Problems* (New York, 1971), 44.

American Collections
on Immigrants and Émigrés
from the Russian Empire

Norman Saul

SUMMARY. The article describes materials on Russian immigrants and immigrant communities in several American collections: the Library of Congress; the University of Chicago; the University of Illinois, Urbana-Champaign; the Hoover Presidential Library in Iowa; and the State Historical Society of Wisconsin. It includes an analysis of immigrations from Russia, relations among various groups, and their influence upon American scholarship on Russia, particularly in regard to American relief efforts in the 1920s. It also examines the records of non-Russian immigrant groups–Mennonites from Ukraine, Germans from the Volga and Black Sea regions, and others. It includes descriptions of archival collections and an account of the contributions of these groups to the economic and social development of the North American Great Plains region. *[Article copies available for a fee from The Haworth Document Delivery Service: 1-800-HAWORTH. E-mail address: <docdelivery@haworthpress.com> Website: <http://www.HaworthPress.com> © 2003 by The Haworth Press, Inc. All rights reserved.]*

Norman Saul, PhD, is Professor of History and of Russian and East European Studies, University of Kansas.

Address correspondence to the author at: Department of History, 1445 Jayhawk Boulevard, University of Kansas, Lawrence, KS 66045 USA (E-mail: normsaul@ku.edu).

[Haworth co-indexing entry note]: "American Collections on Immigrants and Émigrés from the Russian Empire." Saul, Norman. Co-published simultaneously in *Slavic & East European Information Resources* (The Haworth Information Press, an imprint of The Haworth Press, Inc.) Vol. 4, No. 4, 2003, pp. 49-61; and: *Russian and East European Books and Manuscripts in the United States: Proceedings of a Conference in Honor of the Fiftieth Anniversary of the Bakhmeteff Archive of Russian and East European History and Culture* (eds: Tanya Chebotarev and Jared S. Ingersoll) The Haworth Information Press, an imprint of The Haworth Press, Inc., 2003, pp. 49-61. Single or multiple copies of this article are available for a fee from The Haworth Document Delivery Service [1-800-HAWORTH, 9:00 a.m. - 5:00 p.m. (EST). E-mail address: docdelivery@haworthpress.com].

10.1300/J167v04n04_05

KEYWORDS. Russian émigrés, Germans from Russia, immigrants, United States, archives, Mennonites, ethnic relations

The sessions in New York focused on the papers of Russian political and cultural émigrés both before and after 1917 in major American and European collections. Thanks to the variety and quality of the presentations, we now know much more about them and have the potential to discover even more. The Bakhmeteff Archive at Columbia University and the Hoover Institution Archives at Stanford University are the major repositories in the United States, and we owe much to their collectors and archivists for preserving so much of the history of the Russian diaspora.

A question arises, however, about whether these studies belong in the large and growing field of the history of immigration and movements of peoples. The émigrés from Russia, like those from Nazi Germany and other countries with intolerant regimes, were not willing immigrants (though there is also the problem of whether any movement is completely voluntary).[1] These émigrés were really refugees who looked forward to a return to their homeland when conditions allowed. Although some adapted quite well, most never fully accepted their status as permanent residents of another country, settling for nostalgic reminiscences of their past and what might have been. The argument can be easily made, however, that the Russian émigré phenomenon is a definite part of the broader study of the movements of peoples: the whys, hows, and results. The sub-field of Russian movements should include those who were immigrants within Russia, even if they represent non-Slavic populations of the Russian Empire.

In the 1870s a mass migration occurred that transferred a large number of industrious people from Russia to the Central Plains States of North America, one of the longest continuous treks in history. This influx had a profound effect on the economy of the region; America's considerable gain was Russia's loss. Yet this event is almost completely ignored in the general historical literature of both Russia and the United States as well as that on Russian-American relations.

The "Germans from Russia" (including Dutch and Swiss) are historically significant as the first major emigration from Russia in the 1870s, thus establishing a precedent for subsequent migrations. Additionally, they provide a bridge in social analysis for being more comparable to other major immigrations to the United States in the nineteenth and early twentieth centuries, such as the Italians and Irish. They are usually not considered in examinations of the Russian diaspora, yet they had experiences similar to the Russians, Jews, and others leaving Russia:

- They left, often unwillingly, the land that had been theirs for several generations.
- They considered themselves distinctive because of their Russian background and were also treated as different from other Germans by the people where they settled in America.[2]
- They had a major impact upon American society, economy, and politics.
- They reflect the true multinational character of the Russian Empire, an important aspect of the exodus.

The records of the Germans from Russia reveal much about the policies of the Russian government toward non-Slavic peoples and about migration, settlement, and adaptation in general. There is much of interest for the study of emigration and adaptation in the archives of the Dutch- and German-speaking Mennonites who left colonies in Ukraine for the United States and Canada in substantial numbers, beginning in the 1870s. Between 1873 and 1883 over one fourth of Russia's Mennonite population of approximately 100,000 left the steppes of southern Russia to settle on the plains of North America.[3] Many more would follow in later decades. They were relatively prosperous in comparison with other non-Russian immigrant groups such as Jews, Poles, Volga Germans, Ukrainians, Finns, and Armenians and, consequently, adapted both quickly and successfully to their new homeland, economically and socially. Purchasing large tracts of fertile railroad land grants at bargain prices, they made an immediate and lasting impact on American agriculture and society. They represent one of the most notable success stories of nineteenth-century American immigration.

Their archival materials are also unique in providing a comparatively full record of whole colonies in transit, settlement, and adaptation because of their high level of literacy and historical and religious consciousness. Like the Mormons who preceded them across the Plains, they were particularly interested in genealogy and family history, were motivated by economic successes, and kept excellent business records. The church records of the large Alexanderwohl Mennonite Church north of Newton, Kansas, list all births, baptisms, and deaths in the community since it left Friesland (North Holland) in the seventeenth century.[4] The records are also valuable in providing a considerable and almost continuous communication with those Mennonites who remained in Russia, interrupted only by the Stalin era.

In the Mennonite Library and Archives at Bethel College in North Newton are preserved records of churches, the central board of missions (150 cubic feet), relief organizations that focused on Russia, material on the arduous Central Asia trek of the 1880s, and around 400 personal family collections. Among those that are especially revealing for the Russian experience are the papers of Jacob Balzer, Peter Buller, Cornelius Claassen, Heinrich Friesen, Dietrich Gaeddert, David Goertz, Jacob Janzen, Cornelius Krahn, Christian Krehbiel, Abraham Penner, Leonhard Sudermann, Abraham Thiessen, Bernhard Warkentin, and Peter Wiebe.[5]

Subjects in the Mennonite archives include negotiations with the Russian government regarding emigration and/or alternative military service; colonial administration in Russia; difficulties regarding later emigration; internal problems in the Russian colonies; famine relief programs of the 1890s and the 1920s; the search for and the adaptation of hard winter wheat from Ukraine to the Central Plains (Warkentin was a major contribution to the wheat cultivation of the Plains), and the experiences of many tour groups back to the region beginning in the 1950s.[6] Cornelius Krahn, who emigrated from Russia in the 1920s, was a professor of history and founder of this special library and archive at Bethel College in the 1940s.[7] Much published research, based on these and other materials, can be found in the monthly publication, *Mennonite Life*, and in *The Mennonite Historical Quarterly*, edited for many years by Krahn. However, much more remains to be done. How did their effort to aid compatriots in Russia compare with that of other Russian immigrant groups, for example?

The Mennonites from Russia include a number of separate constituencies, such as the Crimean (Krimmer) and the Swiss-Volhynian Mennonites. Those Mennonites who came to Kansas, though living hundreds of miles apart in Southern Russia, settled adjacent to each other. Divided by ethnicity, sectarian orientation, and culture, they have only in recent years developed a more common identity, centered on their Russian experiences. All of these groups were especially interested in education, founded several colleges, and attained quickly and maintain today one of the highest rates of graduation from higher education of any ethnic population in the country. Many entered teaching, medicine, and other professions and are noted for their successes, which facts contribute to a devotion to their own unique history and historical preservation. A model living history museum is located in Goossel, Kansas; the "Adobe House" restoration in Hillsboro and the Kaufman Museum in Newton maintain many early buildings resembling those in their Russian villages and artifacts from Russia. Other collections can be found at major Mennonite centers, such as those in Winnipeg, Manitoba, and Goshen, Indiana.[8]

Another, much larger non-Slavic immigration to America was that of the Volga Germans. Their archival records are not nearly as complete or available as the Mennonites, however, because of their relative poverty, general illiteracy, and the sharp divisions that existed between Roman Catholic and Lutheran denominations. They were also delineated by dialect and the customs of the region from which they originated in eighteenth-century Germany (e.g.,

Hessian, Swabian, Saxon, Bavarian), that fostered rivalry and isolation in both Russia and America. They were also more widely scattered across the central and western United States and Canada. Furthermore, they were divided and distinguished by separate waves of emigration. The first was in the 1870s and early 1880s, just after the Mennonite migration. Like the Mennonites before, this wave also settled primarily on farmland in Kansas, Oklahoma, Minnesota, Nebraska, and Manitoba.[9] The Volga Germans were from a much larger population group (over one million) than the Mennonites, and the immigration was consequently larger and more scattered.

A second exodus occurred in the 1890s, composed mostly of more Russified but quite destitute famine refugees, who could not afford to buy land. They settled in prairie towns such as Topeka, Lincoln, and Fort Collins and Greeley in Colorado, and worked in mills, on the railroads, and as farm hands in the northern Colorado sugar beet fields. They continued to constitute a large portion of emigration from Russia into the early twentieth century and are now a permanent fixture in the western half of the United States. Finally, many of those who remained in Russia, forcibly deported to Kazakhstan during World War II, began to trickle out in the 1970s, becoming nearly a flood more recently. Most of them, however, went to Germany because of U.S. immigration restrictions.

The records of the Volga Germans are less complete and more scattered than for the Mennonites, but some projects are underway. The American Historical Society of Germans from Russia (AHSGR) in Lincoln has promoted the formation of many separate chapters in the central and western states that are quite active, such as holding Octoberfests, an adopted German-American custom. The AHSGR holds annual "international" conventions that draw hundreds of participants.[10] At its beginning primarily concentrated on Lutheran Volga Germans, this organization quickly expanded to include Roman Catholics and more recently many Mennonites from Russia, becoming quite ecumenical. Besides the headquarters museum and library in Lincoln and a small archive in Greeley, Colorado, most chapters have their own small collections of memorabilia, which may include valuable historical documents.[11] Evidently, an inventory of these materials is very much needed.

Centers of scholarly study and collections of sources on the Volga Germans have been initiated at Colorado State University in Fort Collins, at Portland State University in Oregon, and at North Dakota State University in Fargo,[12] and more recently at the University of Kansas.[13] A wealth of new information on the Volga Germans in the United States is both historic and current but is, admittedly, rather amateurish. Much of it can be found in the long run of the journal of AHSGR, published quarterly for the past twenty-five years.[14] Librarians, archivists, and faculty should be encouraged to lend their expertise to these endeavors.

A third major Russian-German immigrant group in America is the Black Sea and Bessarabian Germans from the Odessa region and present-day Moldova, who settled mainly in North and South Dakota in the 1880s and 1890s. Much less is known about their archives and recordkeeping, but the Germans from Russia Heritage Society, headquartered in Bismarck, has published many first-hand accounts of life in Russia and on the immigration and settlement in America in its *Heritage Review*. They, too, according to their website (http://www.grhs.com/), are starting a major collection effort of manuscript material. With much more of a regional concentration in the Dakotas, the Black Sea Germans, nevertheless, have their own diaspora story and experiences under Russian administration.

Unfortunately, little about these Mennonite and German immigrant exiles from Russia and their records and publications is known in wider academic circles. What is especially needed is a broader network for the collection and distribution of information about archival holdings. Such a network might logically be centered at Columbia University and the New York Public Library. Many of the original manuscripts, published but not preserved in a public collection, may be lost in the transfer or nontransfer from one generation to the next, but certainly a retrieval effort is of paramount importance not only in preserving the records that survived of their experiences, but also for the much-needed comparative study of Russian emigration. And there are still many family records that have not been published or collected. Others with Russian heritage are important and equally diffuse but ignored: Lithuanians, Poles, Georgians, Armenians, or those with regional identities such as Siberians. All had common, yet interestingly different, experiences.

Perhaps the first step should be to establish a network of contacts with civic leaders, individual archivists, librarians, and journal editors (most of whom have websites and e-mail addresses) with the goal of creating a new, more comprehensive online information center that would not be confined just to Russian émigrés, but to the experiences and archival resources of the total, much larger, and more varied diaspora. Though an appreciation of the influence and contributions of these non-Slavic immigrant/exiles from Russia to the American economy and society is recognized in their regions, it should be realized or appreciated by specialists on the Russian diaspora and scholars of immigration studies.[15]

RUSSIAN ÉMIGRÉ SOURCES IN AMERICAN COLLECTIONS

The main currents of Russian émigré history and their archival resources are associated with and dependent on, individual Americans who had extensive interests in Russia through travel, business, study and writing. Some of these, such as Charles R. Crane, have already been discussed but still need more scholarly investigation and general attention.[16] A number of other Americans, like Crane, contributed immensely to an understanding of Russian culture in America and to the Russian émigré welfare and experience. It was a two-way street. While a number of Americans, such as Charles Crane and George Kennan, were enamored of so many things Russian, Russians abroad especially cultivated Americans, not only for the money that might be forthcoming, but for the ideological bonding toward a democratic future. Much material on this unique guest/host relationship remains to be investigated.

In such an examination of major American collections outside the Bakhmeteff and Hoover archives,[17] one must begin with George Kennan, who lived and traveled in Siberia and wrote and lectured extensively about his experiences, informing vast numbers of ordinary Americans about Russia and especially regarding Russians pursuing an anti-autocratic cause. The most important collection of his papers pertaining to Russian exiles and émigrés over a long period of the nineteenth and early twentieth centuries is in the Library of Congress Manuscript Division.[18] Other smaller manuscript sources are in the New York Public Library and at the University of Rochester.

Kennan was a copious notetaker, diarist, and avid file clerk, who believed in using pencil only, insisting that lead would preserve as well as ink, could be corrected, and would not smear. True, his pencil marks hold up well over time, but, unfortunately, skinflint as he was, he wrote on the cheapest paper he could find, and much of it is now disintegrating. To read his letters and especially his valuable and irreplaceable notes on Siberian exiles, which are enclosed in equally fragile envelopes, one must start as with a jigsaw puzzle, piecing parts together. This is not an easy task, especially when several pages are included in a single folder or envelope. A major preservation project is required immediately to preserve this valuable source on Russian exiles and émigrés and make it more readily available to researchers.[19] Most of the Kennan papers, however, relate to the pre-1917 generation of political exiles and émigrés, few of whom settled in the United States permanently but, like Ekaterina Breshko-Breshkovskaia, preferred Europe instead.

Comparable to the Kennan Papers are those of Isabel Hapgood, prolific translator of Russian novels and commentator on Russian life, in the manuscript collection of the New York Public Library. As a friend of Leo Tolstoy and other writers, she naturally had many Russian contacts, and kept material relating to them, though much less well organized than Kennan's. Unfortunately, few of the papers of two other contemporary American experts on Russia, Archibald Cary Coolidge, professor of history at Harvard University, and Nathan Haskell Dole, seem to have survived.[20]

Perhaps the most important American collection on Russian émigré history is that of Samuel Harper, the founder of Russian Studies at the University of Chicago. Harper, unlike Kennan, relied on the typewriter, but similar problems occur in regard to the legibility of dim carbon copies of his outgoing correspondence.[21] He did, however, preserve practically everything over a long period of time–the first half of the twentieth century–so that his papers are a real treasure of the history of Russian-American relations for that period. They describe the experiences of prominent Russians in America, especially Pavel Miliukov and Sergei Obolenskii, but also many others, including those remaining in Europe. Harper's position as a consultant to the State Department and his sponsorship by Charles Crane add additional weight to the value of the correspondence. The papers also provide a chronology of an American scholar's shift from firm opposition to Bolshevism and an ardent opponent of diplomatic recognition to a more sympathetic and pro-recognition stance by the early 1930s.[22]

Harper began his intensive study of Russia and the Russian language just after the 1905 revolution on a mandate (actually a written contract dictated by his father, William Rainey Harper), to learn Russian. This mandate was initially financed by Charles Crane, who had introduced the elder Harper to Leo Tolstoy on a visit to Russia in 1900 and converted him to the cause of expanding an appreciation of Russian culture in academic America.[23] The Crane-Harper connection and its contribution to Russian-American émigré studies certainly need more investigation and appreciation. The Harper Papers are well organized and expertly superintended, one of the best to work with, yet remain generally neglected in the literature on Russian émigré-American relations.

During his sojourns in Russia over several summers preceding World War I, Samuel Harper obtained fluency in Russian. He became closely associated with the moderate liberal opposition forces in Russia headed by Pavel Miliukov, who, under auspices of Harper-Crane sponsorship, lectured at the University of Chicago and elsewhere in America. The associated publicity contributed to strong American support for the liberal cause in Russia and to disillusionment in its ultimate failure in 1917. Harper's papers, therefore, include much material on the Russian liberal experience in Russia and in exile. They record the details of his activities in Russia as chief advisor to Ambassador Francis in 1917, his role as a key advisor to the State Department after the Revolution, and his work as a special State Department advisor on Russian affairs, a function which also involved the departures of many Russian refugees from war and revolution. Much of this activity can also be credited to regular annual contributions from Charles Crane to the university and specifically to his university contract, library supplements, lecture funds, and salary.[24] Even then, it was not easy to maintain a program of Russian Studies without outside support.

Several other Americans established close personal contacts with Russians, more so perhaps than any other nation. Again, Crane's financial promotion played a major role. Elizabeth Reynolds was a young New York socialite who was won over to a dedication to Russian language, literature, and culture by a Russian émigré-exile in New York, Zenaide Ragozin, a prolific author, historian, artist, musician–and eccentric–of the Russian nineteenth century diaspora. This remarkable woman represents an unusual duality: a Russian exile in America for twenty-five years, from around 1875 to 1900, and then an American exile in Russia for the next quarter century until her death in 1924. She excelled as a tutor of foreign language, music, art, and history to a generation of New York debutantes, which included the Pulitzer, Tiffany, and Putnam families.[25]

Through Ragozin's close friendship with her mother, Elizabeth Reynolds became Ragozin's favorite protégée and student in Russian arts and letters. Ragozin encouraged Elizabeth Reynolds's study of Russian language and literature during extended summer sojourns in Russia. Reynolds then formalized it by professional study with Paul Boyer in Paris in 1913-14. The extensive correspondence between Margaret and Elizabeth Reynolds and Zenaide Ragozin, her friends, relatives, and associates is quite remarkable in its coverage of a vital period of Russian cultural and political history from 1900, when Ragozin returned to Russia, until her death in 1924.

This extraordinary Zenaide-Elizabeth correspondence is "hidden away" in the Norman Hapgood Papers at the Library of Congress.[26] Hapgood, editor of *Harpers Weekly* (coincidentally owned by Crane) met Reynolds when she became an instructor of Russian language and literature at Columbia University in 1915. Despite a wide difference in age, their marriage in 1916 was apparently quite successful. Her vivacity, intelligence, and beauty attracted the attention and sponsorship of Crane and the attention of New York society. She thus became another key member of a dynamic Crane Russian circle. Other relevant information in the wider Reynolds-Ragozin circle can be found in other collections, such as those of George Putnam at Columbia University and in Pushkinskii Dom in St. Petersburg, where a small Ragozin collection is archived. Due to Norman Hapgood's position as a respected New York theater critic and Elizabeth's interests in Russian language and literature, they became the cosponsors of the visits of Konstantin Stanislavsky and the Moscow Art Theater to New York in the 1920s and the translators of all of his work into English. The English rights to Stanislavsky's works still reside in the Hapgood estate.[27]

A number of other papers of Americans relate to Russian émigrés in the United States and Europe. These include Alice Stone Blackwell, a prominent American feminist, who sponsored the travels, lectures, and political contacts of Breshko-Breshkovskaia and Maria Bochkareva during their tours of the United States during the revolutionary era. Much more information about the American assistance to the large waves of Russian refugees from the Revolution and Civil War are in a number of American collections, especially that of Mark and Helen Bristol and Newton McCully. Admiral Bristol was the High Commissioner for the former Ottoman Empire, Commander of the U.S. Mediterranean fleet, and head of the American Red Cross during the mass exodus of Russian refugees that occurred in November 1920.[28] He and his staff devoted their energies and American resources to a gigantic rescue effort and the subsequent resettlement of thousands of Russians in Europe and the United States. Their commitment to Russian émigré relief and those of many other officers, especially Admiral Newton McCully, who (though a bachelor) adopted seven Russian orphans while on duty in the Black Sea, did not end in 1920, but continued throughout the inter-war period. This story has not really been told. The Bristols were especially influential in securing the admission of Russian academics such as historians Michael Florinsky, George Vernadsky, and many other "Russian professors" to the United States.

Because of immigration restrictions, American admission of Russians after the Revolution was selective, allowing only those with professional expertise valued in the United States or individuals who could help preserve the best of Russian culture abroad. But there were also many marginal cases that allowed some families to "sneak under the wire." Americans thus contributed on a larger scale to the cause of assisting young Russians, in pursuit of the performance arts and to study at American universities, chiefly in technical and engineering fields. The records of the "Russian Student Fund" in the University Archives of the University of Illinois are a valuable reservoir of the operations of an ambitious philanthropic endeavor that continued into the 1950s.[29]

Thanks to Ralph Fisher, the University of Illinois preserves the records of individual YMCA secretaries who had extensive experience in the Russia of war and revolution and in refugee relief (for example, Paul Anderson, Donald Lowrie, and Helen Ogden). Of special interest to the Russian émigré community after the Revolution was the work of the American YMCA in Western Europe, headed by Anderson in Berlin, who developed systematic courses of study for Russian refugees in Western Europe and helped them adjust to the new environment and secure employment. A special program of the YMCA press there and later in Paris published many of their works in Russian, some of which were aimed at those remaining in Russia–textbooks on a variety of subjects.

Finally, many Americans had sporadic contact with the Russian exiles because they held key positions in and out of government. Prominent among these were Assistant Secretary of State Breckinridge Long; Herbert Hoover, famous for his World War I refugee work and head of the American Relief Administration; Frank Golder, Hoover's personal agent in Russia and first director of the Hoover Institution at Stanford University; Jerome Landfield, a professor at the University of California at Berkeley and a newspaper editor, who served briefly in the State Department, and whose wife was Russian; J. Butler Wright, first secretary in the embassy in Petrograd in 1917; Robert F. Kelley, head of the East European Division of the State Department; and Father Edmund Walsh, founder of the School of Foreign Policy at Georgetown University.[30]

In conclusion, perhaps a broader conception of the Russian diaspora in the United States and American contributions to it is in order. The large number of Russians who opposed the autocracy and later Bolshevik-Communist dictatorship were supported and assisted by sympathetic Americans, such as George Kennan, Breckinridge Long, Isabel Hapgood, Alice Stone Blackwell, Paul Anderson, Charles Crane, Samuel Harper, Elizabeth Reynolds, Mark and Helen Bristol, and many others. These Russian-American interconnections, a major part of the story of the Russian diaspora, deserve more research and investigation. In America they were able to continue to explore those eternal Russian questions: whither Russia–and what is to be done? The preservation of those records and the answers to the questions they raise are a vital legacy of the Russian-American experience in the twentieth century. Émigré Russians in America were vital in preserving and fostering the richness of Russia's cultural heritage and the resurrection of the real Russia, the importance of which is perhaps yet to be fully revealed.

NOTES

1. Many of immigrants did, in fact, return. See Mark K. Wyman, *Round Trip to America: The Immigrants Return to Europe, 1880-1930* (Ithaca, NY: Cornell University Press, 1993).

2. When they arrived in Topeka, Lincoln, and other Central Plains towns, they were asked where they were from and immediately answered, "Rooshia." They became known then and until now as "Rooshians." An area of settlement in Topeka, Kansas, is still referred to as "Little Russia" and a similar one in Lincoln, Nebraska, as "Russian Bottoms."

3. See the classic C. Henry Smith, *The Coming of the Russian Mennonites: An Episode in the Settling of the Last Frontier: 1874-1884* (Berne, IN: Mennonite Book Concern, 1927). Though long out of print and obviously dated, this is still the best source on the subject. For an updated survey, see Norman E. Saul, "The Migration of the Rus-

sian-Germans to Kansas," *The Kansas Historical Quarterly* 40, no. 1 (Spring 1974): 38-63. They also captured American attention as perhaps no other Russian immigrant or émigré group did. See *Frank Leslie's Illustrated Newspaper*, 20 March 1875.

4. The church is the largest wooden church, built in Dutch amphitheater design, in the Central Plains. The original books are kept in the basement vault with microfilm copies available in several other locations.

5. See the Mennonite Library and Archives website <http://www.bethelks.edu/services/mla/> (16 June 2003) for more information on the archive.

6. For a description by a physician who participated in eight of these tours, see Wilmer A. Harms, "The Story of My Tours to the Ukraine," *Journal of the American Historical Society of Germans from Russia* 24, no. 2 (Summer 2001): 5-8.

7. Cornelius Krahn, ed., *From the Steppes to the Prairies: 1874-1949* (Newton, KS: Mennonite Publication Office, 1949).

8. For details, see the various websites and past issues of *Mennonite Life, Mennonite Historical Quarterly*, and *The Mennonite Historical Bulletin.*

9. The leading background sources are the late German historian Karl Stumpp, *The German-Russians: Two Centuries of Pioneering*, trans. Joseph Height (Bonn, Germany: Atlantic-Forum, 1967); A. A. Klaus, *Nashi kolonii: opyty i materialy po istorii i statistike inostrannoi kolonizatsii v Rossii* (Our Colonies: Experiences and Materials on the History and Statistics of Foreign Colonization in Russia) (St. Petersburg: Nusvalt, 1869); and Adam Giesinger, *From Catherine to Khrushchev: The Story of Russia's Germans* (Winnepeg, Canada: Giesinger, 1974). The major archive for the Volga Germans is in Stuttgart, the Institut für Ausländische Deutsche. A sizeable microfilm copy of the section of it relating to the Volga German Republic of the 1920s is available in the Max Kade Center at the University of Kansas.

10. The most recent, the 32nd, was held in June 2000 in Denver.

11. For a partial listing, see Adam Giesinger et al. comps., *Bibliography of the AHSGR Archives and Historical Library, Greeley, Colorado* (Lincoln: The Society, 1976).

12. Probably the leading academic scholar on the Volga Germans in the United States is Timothy Kloberdanz of North Dakota State University, but he is primarily a sociologist and folklorist. Much new and interesting historical research is emanating from universities in Saratov in recent years and has been translated into English by Richard Rye of AHSGR.

13. This project is planned to focus on the inventory and retrieval of the records of the Volga German colony in Russia, mainly in Saratov, but it is dependent on funding.

14. *Journal of the American Historical Society of Germans from Russia*, 631 D Street, Lincoln, Nebraska 68502 USA. The volume of memoirs, diaries, and letters concerning emigration, famine, revolution, civil war, collectivization, and deportation–important sources on twentieth-century Russia submitted by descendants–is certainly impressive. Unfortunately, many of the original manuscripts (letters, diaries, and memoirs) published in this journal may have been lost for lack of a systematic preservation effort.

15. Much current research has focused on the role of immigration and ethnicity in American history, but the enormous contribution of the many immigrants from Russia has been almost totally ignored or misrepresented in American immigration studies.

16. Besides the Crane Papers, the Bakhmeteff Archive holds the papers of Allen Wardwell, Ernest Ropes, and Graham Taylor, Jr. In addition to Boris Bakhmeteff's own papers, those of Michael Florinsky, Geroid Robinson, and Dmitri Fedotoff-White

are especially valuable for Russian-American interconnections. The papers of Charles Crane's son Richard at Georgetown University are also an important complement to those at Columbia University.

17. Bakhmeteff and Hoover collections are large repositories that contain neglected materials of many Americans who had some relation to Russia, for example, those of Thomas Thacher in the Bakhmeteff Archive.

18. These papers include diaries, notebooks, letters, and a large file of resource notes on Siberian exiles. George Kennan Papers, Manuscript Division, Library of Congress.

19. This material would be a prime candidate for digitization.

20. Ironically, because of quarrels over translations and political viewpoints, Kennan, Hapgood, Coolidge, and Dole had virtually no contact with each other.

21. Samuel Harper Papers, Special Collections, Regenstein Library, University of Chicago. Harper also was a skinflint and apparently used carbons to the limit.

22. See also his memoirs, *Russia As I See It*, Samuel Harper Papers, University of Chicago.

23. The handling of the finances came from a special "Friendship" fund of over a million dollars that was superintended by Crane's manager, Roger Williams. Harper drew on this money for such special needs as travel expenses.

24. Much information is in the Harper Papers about the financing of Russian Studies at the University of Chicago and elsewhere, which included funds for lectures and library purchases.

25. Another neglected Russian émigré source in terms of reporting on America in Russia and Russia in America is Barbara Macgahan, widow of the "first American war correspondent" (Russo-Turkish War), who wrote extensively for both Russian and American newspapers, while resident in America from the 1870s to the early 1900s. Unfortunately, few of her private papers survive, and they are mostly in family possession.

26. The Hapgood Papers, Manuscript Division, Library of Congress.

27. Besides the Hapgood Papers in the Library of Congress, there is also an Elizabeth Hapgood collection on her relationships with Konstantin Stanislavsky in the Billy Rose Theater Collection at the New York Public Library at Lincoln Center.

28. The Bristol papers (Manuscript Division, Library of Congress) illustrate a not uncommon feature of archival holdings in America, that many official records were retained in private hands. So much of the story of official American relief of the Russian émigré diaspora must be sought outside of the domain of official papers, and much of this material may have been lost.

29. Russian Student Fund, University of Illinois Archives. The curator, Aleksei Viren, was the son of the last imperial commander of the Kronstadt naval base and one of the first victims of the February Revolution.

30. The extensive Hoover materials are divided between the Hoover Institution and the presidential library in West Branch, Iowa; Golder's are in the Hoover Institution Archive; Long's in the Manuscript Division, Library of Congress; Wright's in the Seeley Mudd Library at Princeton University; and Kelley's and Walsh's are preserved in Special Collections at Georgetown University.

The New York Public Library's Émigré Readership and Collections: Past, Present, and Future

Robert H. Davis, Jr.

SUMMARY. This paper provides a broad overview of the history of the New York Public Library's collections, and most particularly of the NYPL's changing relationship with the city's diverse émigré communities over the past 104 years. The focus of collections has changed over the years with the population served, as have the library's strategies for serving user needs. Also discussed are preservation projects, the effects of economic crises on the collections, and new technological initiatives. *[Article copies available for a fee from The Haworth Document Delivery Service: 1-800-HAWORTH. E-mail address: <docdelivery@haworthpress.com> Website: <http://www.HaworthPress.com> © 2003 by The Haworth Press, Inc. All rights reserved.]*

KEYWORDS. New York Public Library, Russian émigrés, Slavs, libraries, Slavic collections, immigrants, Slavic librarians, United States

Robert H. Davis, Jr. is Senior Librarian for Special Collections and Outreach, Slavic and Baltic Division, The New York Public Library, Fifth Avenue and 42nd Street, New York, NY 10018-2788 USA (E-mail: rdavis@nypl.org).

The author wishes to thank Edward Kasinec and Marc Raeff for their insightful commentary on this and other papers at the Bakhmeteff Conference.

[Haworth co-indexing entry note]: "The New York Public Library's Émigré Readership and Collections: Past, Present, and Future." Davis, Jr., Robert H. Co-published simultaneously in *Slavic & East European Information Resources* (The Haworth Information Press, an imprint of The Haworth Press, Inc.) Vol. 4, No. 4, 2003, pp. 63-75; and: *Russian and East European Books and Manuscripts in the United States: Proceedings of a Conference in Honor of the Fiftieth Anniversary of the Bakhmeteff Archive of Russian and East European History and Culture* (eds: Tanya Chebotarev and Jared S. Ingersoll) The Haworth Information Press, an imprint of The Haworth Press, Inc., 2003, pp. 63-75. Single or multiple copies of this article are available for a fee from The Haworth Document Delivery Service [1-800-HAWORTH, 9:00 a.m. - 5:00 p.m. (EST). E-mail address: docdelivery@haworthpress.com].

The growth and historical significance of research collections devoted to the study of the Slavic, Baltic, East European, and Eurasian emigrations was a central theme of the conference held at the Bakhmeteff Archive. Since the late nineteenth century, the New York Public Library (NYPL) has had a leading role in collecting and describing vernacular Slavic and East European language materials to a diverse readership. Not surprisingly, this role has evolved over time and at no time more rapidly than over the past decade. The following text provides a broad overview of the history of the collections, and most particularly of the NYPL's changing relationship with New York's diverse émigré communities over the past 104 years.

FIRST PERIOD: 1850s-1898

The history of the NYPL's Slavic and East European collections predates the founding of the NYPL itself in 1895.[1] Both the Astor Library (founded 1848) and the Lenox Library (founded 1870), "parent" collections of the NYPL, collected materials pertaining to the history and peoples of Eastern and Central Europe. Although most of the materials were in English and other Roman-script, non-Slavic languages, travel accounts and ethnographic works were especially widely obtained. Nevertheless, this material provided a core of pertinent–and, for American libraries, exceedingly rare–material for the future NYPL. Although European booksellers were the source for most of these titles, such as the seventeenth-century travelog by Adam Olearius, or the eighteenth-century description and history of Russia by Nicolas Le Clerc, some of the rarest items were presented by highly placed individuals in foreign governments. In 1864, for example, Alexander II presented James Lenox (via the Russian Consul General) a facsimile of the *Codex Sinaiticus* (St. Petersburg, 1862), while his son Alexander III gave the Astor Library *Antiquités de Bosphore Cimmérien* (St. Petersburg, 1854) in 1882. Slavic and Baltic vernacular materials, however, were infrequently used well into the nineteenth century, with the occasional, short-lived burst of interest.

SECOND PERIOD: 1898-1958

By the late 1890s, emigration from Eastern and Central Europe–particularly, well-educated Jewish professionals and intellectuals–had reached a sufficiently critical mass that demands were made on the newly founded NYPL to include materials in Slavic languages. In 1899, the library's first director, Dr. John Shaw Billings, received a petition signed by fifty-eight members of the

Russian-speaking émigré community: " . . . desirous of promoting the knowl-edge of Russia, her literature, history, institutions and social life, among the American Public . . . "[2] Their petition convinced the Trustees to establish a Russian department, which soon broadened in scope to become the Slavonic Division. In the closing decade of the nineteenth century up to the outbreak of World War I, the collections grew rapidly through a combination of gifts from the émigré community, purchase, and exchange with libraries and learned so-cieties in Eastern Europe. Herman Rosenthal, the first chief of these collec-tions, worked tirelessly to cultivate relationships with overseas institutions for the exchange of publications. Russophone political exiles, primarily Social Democrats (including Lev Deich, Dovid Shub, Nikolai Bukharin, and Lev Trotsky) became avid users of the collections, which provided access not only to literature banned at home, but also to works on economic and social history pertaining to other countries.[3] By 1917 the collection numbered some 25,000 Slavic vernacular-language volumes, predominantly in Russian. As the collec-tions expanded, so did readership, growing from 1,240 patrons in 1900 to 19,500 in 1916.[4] When the Library of Congress purchased the 80,000-volume Yudin Collection in 1906, it could rightly claim by far the largest Russian ver-nacular collection in the nation. However, many of these volumes were uncataloged and the collection was therefore largely inaccessible to readers for decades to come. Furthermore, Washington lacked the Slavic-speaking read-ership of New York, so the Library of Congress's collections remained un-der-processed and under-utilized, and received neither the diversity nor the quantity of gifts made by NYPL readers. The NYPL system had in the mean-time become the world's busiest, and its Slavic collections were no exception.

In addition to the non-circulating research collection in the Slavonic Divi-sion, the NYPL's extensive network of branch libraries served the city's Slavic-speaking communities. The branch libraries of the NYPL have a long and progressive tradition of reaching out to ethnic communities and religious and fraternal organizations in the neighborhoods they have served. In the early decades of the twentieth century, Manhattan branches such as the Hamilton Fish Park (East Houston Street), 96th Street, Seward Park (East Broadway), and old Rivington Street, as well as the Tremont (Washington Avenue) in the Bronx, all circulated Russian-language materials. Polish books were available in Manhattan's Tompkins Square (First Avenue) and Columbus Branches (Tenth Avenue), and in the Bronx's Melrose (Morris Avenue) Branch.[5] In 1909, when the NYPL included only some forty branch libraries (today there are 84), the 3,405 Czech, 443 Polish, and 2,885 Russian volumes held by the branch libraries circulated among 24,658, 3,085, and 26,292 readers, respec-tively–fully 16 percent of the total foreign-language readership of the entire system.[6] Five years later, in 1914, Slavic circulating collections included

"3,525 Bohemian, 20,590 Russian, 1,331 Polish, 157 Slovak, and 70 Serbian titles, while Ruthenian [i.e., Ukrainian] was a new language added during the past year."[7]

The story of the NYPL's Webster Branch, situated in the Yorkville neighborhood of Manhattan, is a remarkable example of collection-building and service to an immigrant community–in this case, the Czech and Slovak enclave of the Upper East Side. As early as 1911, it published *Bohemian Book List*, the first known NYPL publication devoted to Slavic materials. By the early 1920s, the 15,000 volumes in the Webster Branch constituted the largest Czech and Slovak vernacular-language library outside Czechoslovakia. More than a library, the Webster Branch served as a cultural center as well, organizing exhibits of posters, costume, and handicrafts, and presenting musical performances and lecture series. So great was its contribution to the Czech and Slovak diaspora that in 1927 the library was awarded the Order of the White Lion in recognition of its efforts. In a pattern that has been repeated again and again, when the Czech and Slovak community assimilated and moved away, in the early 1960s the Webster's circulating Slavic holdings were ultimately transferred to the non-circulating collections of the Slavic and Baltic Division, and to the World Languages Collection at the Donnell Library, a Central Branch.[8]

The year 1917 marked the beginning of an extended period of spectacular growth in the NYPL's Slavic, Baltic, and East European collections, under the masterful eye of Avrahm Tsalevich Yarmolinsky, himself an immigrant and Columbia's first Ph.D. in Slavic literatures. Over the next thirty-nine years, until his retirement in 1956, Yarmolinsky built one of the most important research collections for Slavic studies, and particularly Russian studies, in North America. Throughout his tenure, support and creative criticism from the émigré communities were absolutely crucial in terms of acquisitions; staffing; and, of course, readership, which ballooned to more than 40,000 per year during the mid-1920s.

The wave of immigration following World War I, the 1917 Revolution, and the subsequent Russian Civil War brought many highly educated individuals to the United States, often via the émigré centers of Paris, Berlin, and Prague. Once settled, many joined and revitalized existing fraternal and cultural organizations or formed new groups of their own. To foster their own activities, these groups, in turn, used their international contacts to provide the library with much valuable material, produced both in the homelands and in emigration. In 1919, for example, the library received large numbers of underground pamphlets and periodicals produced by revolutionary groups of various tendencies, including an entire convoy of materials gathered by a New York socialist organization. In contrast to the collection's first decades, readership in the interwar period was large–some 40,000 readers in 1924 alone–and far more varied ethnically and politically. Tales abound of how Mensheviks glared across the tables in the reading room at Bolsheviks, and Whites glared at both. Yet this emotionally charged atmosphere, coupled with Yarmolinsky's emphasis on developing a broadly based collection rich in both prerevolutionary and current materials helped to produce the remarkable resource available today.

American-born scholars and researchers on Slavic and East European issues were still rare in the interwar years. The 1920s saw the passing of what may be considered the first generation of such specialists–figures such as George Kennan, and Isabel F. Hapgood–and the younger generation was small in numbers as well. Readers remained predominantly immigrants and the mature children of immigrants.

It is a little known fact that Avrahm Yarmolinsky presciently anticipated the need for and initiated the creation of a kind of resource similar to what the Bakhmeteff Archive has become, and well before the latter became a reality on Columbia's campus. Shortly after the fall of Paris, in his 1940 *Annual Report of the Slavonic Division*, Yarmolinsky wrote the following:

> To systematize and enlarge the work of collecting fugitive literature and unpublished records of the Russian Dispersion, as well as to secure any manuscripts relating to recent Russian history which may be in private hands, the Russian Historical Archives in the United States were established in connection with the Division. An effort was also made to popularize the idea that the Library is a suitable depository for similar material in Polish and Czech.[9]

He subsequently succeeded in securing donations of a number of such collections, which now reside in the Manuscripts Division of the NYPL. Among these are the unpublished memoirs, diaries, and letters of Michael Riabouchinsky, covering the period 1917-60; the papers of the Federation of Russian Organizations in America (1918-24); and Miriam Shoner Zunser's papers (1900-07), documenting Jewish life under the last three tsars. Yarmolinsky also had the foresight to have photostatic reproductions made of important research materials in private hands, including three leaves of a thirteenth-century Slavic manuscript. The postwar establishment of the Bakhmeteff Archive, devoted to collecting and organizing manuscript and archival materials, diminished the need for the primarily book-oriented Slavonic Division to pursue its "Russian Historical Archives" initiative further.

Immigration during both the immediate prewar years and after 1945 assisted collection development and brought thousands of new émigré readers to the library. Obviously, the life experiences of many of these new émigrés were far different from their interwar predecessors, many of whom straddled the old and new regimes. However, as a group they were no less concerned about the fate of their fellow countrymen. Both those who left the Soviet Union as displaced persons and those who saw homelands lose their independence were passionate in their desire to follow events overseas, while building and documenting their communities' new lives in emigration. A glance at *The Directory of American Organizations of Exiles from the USSR* (New York, 1952), for example, suggests the postwar diversity of fraternal, religious, military, professional, political, and social welfare organizations situated in New York and New Jersey. The *Directory* indicates that in 1952, New York's five boroughs were home to seventy-six Russian secular organizations, from the Russian Free Theater on West 96th Street and the Union of Russian Judiciary Abroad at 170 Broadway, to Brooklyn's Society of New Russian Immigrants in the USA. The NYPL, as before, continued to collect intensively materials from both the diaspora and the Communist-controlled homelands.

THIRD PERIOD: 1958-1991

In 1960, Melville J. Ruggles and Vaclav Mostecky published the results of a two-year study of Russian and East European resources in the United States.[10] It not only provided a detailed qualitative and quantitative overview and analysis of the status of relevant area studies' collections, but also reviewed some of the myriad difficulties then facing librarians and bibliographers. The study determined that although quantitatively the Library of Congress continued to far surpass all other libraries surveyed, from a qualitative standpoint, Harvard, NYPL, Columbia, and the Library of Congress were deemed of equal value to the research community, each with particular strengths. They were essentially complimentary, collectively forming a significant resource base for North American library researchers.

The immediate post-World War II period saw the creation of Slavic studies centers, most notably at Columbia and Harvard Universities. These entities provided an organizational center for the coordination of area studies education. The ranks of academic specialists on Eastern and Central Europe were swelled both by Americans trained in Slavic languages during military service and by many postwar émigrés. However, it was only after the launch of Sputnik that the federal government began to inject significant sums of money into both training programs and library resources centers for academic programs in area studies where previously none had existed or were small-scale. The University of Illinois at Urbana-Champaign is the preeminent example, growing from a mere 1,790 Slavic vernacular volumes in 1946 to become the largest collection west of the Mississippi with some half million volumes by the early 1970s. Much of the collection development of such institutions was focused on current acquisitions. Illinois and others also intensively developed pre-Soviet holdings through the purchase or exchange of microforms, selections from exchange partners' duplicate stocks in Eastern Europe, and from antiquarian dealers such as George Sabo and Israel Perlstein.

The purpose of such collections is to make possible understanding of the current regimes from a variety of historical, cultural, and socio-political perspectives. It is worth recalling that most academic libraries and programs focused almost exclusively on materials from the homelands, and particularly those from the Russian Republic. The lives and writings of those who left, with the exception of a few literary and academic luminaries, were largely marginalized in university and college libraries and programs. The personal political beliefs of American-born faculty and students, particularly during the domestic political turmoil of the 1960s and 1970s, frequently colored attitudes towards émigrés of the first and second waves, and even towards the national aspirations of minority peoples of the Soviet Union.

Throughout the 1960s and 1970s, readership in the Slavonic Division remained high but became more evenly divided between academic (students and faculty) and émigré readers. Social and political historians, in particular, populated the reading room, because their home institutions still lacked the depth and breadth of the NYPL's Slavic and East European resources.

Unfortunately, aside from a modest level of participation in the PL-480 acquisitions program, during the 1960s, 1970s, and early 1980s the NYPL failed to pursue actively foundation- and government-funded Cold War initiatives for libraries. The collections still grew on the basis of longstanding exchange relationships, yet opportunities were missed to expand staffing and to enhance retrospective collections dramatically (or replace deteriorating hardcopy) through the purchase of commercially available microforms.

In the 1970s the economy of the city of New York deteriorated to the point of crisis. Although funding for the research libraries of the NYPL is derived from a combination of endowment income through the private Astor, Lenox, and Tilden Foundation, the city operates and maintains the library's buildings and provides significant support for other activities, particularly those involving the branch libraries. Rampant inflation significantly reduced the buying power of the budget, and a prolonged down market suppressed endowment income, creating profound uncertainty about the long-term viability of the institution. Library-wide attempts to cut costs included the adoption of collection-curtailment guidelines in the late 1970s and early 1980s. The Serials Reduction Project, for example, cut the number of current periodical subscriptions in the Slavic and Baltic Division alone from 1,153 in 1978 to 982 in 1981. Artificially priced Soviet and Eastern Europe imprints continued to flow in, but processing was indefinitely deferred, resulting in large cataloging backlogs. By 1974, Division heads were instructed not to purchase "antiquarian" materials, defined as anything published in Europe before 1970![11]

The local and national fiscal crisis of the 1970s had a particularly negative impact on the acquisition of émigré materials, which were purchased. However, through the cooperation of émigré organizations, during the 1970s and early 1980s the NYPL still acquired current and retrospective émigré materials. Newspapers issued by Boston's Latvian community, the proceedings of various Ukrainian fraternal organizations, large sets of Carpatho-Rusyn serials on microfilm, and the publisher's complete backfiles of major newspapers like *New Yorské listy*, all came to the NYPL through the efforts of metropolitan area fraternal and religious organizations. Such efforts sometimes took the form of a barter relationship, in which the organization would provide backfiles in exchange for microfilm copy.

The survival of the Slavonic Division through the fiscal crisis of the 1970s is owed at least in part to the efforts of the late Viktor Koressaar, the fifth chief.[12] His successor, Edward Kasinec, has led the collections of the division through a period of tremendous growth and activity.

Kasinec, a reader in the division since 1966, began his tenure as curator in 1984, during the presidency of the dynamic Vartan Gregorian. Gregorian brought the library back to the attention of New York philanthropists, and oversaw a thorough renovation of much of the landmark facility on Fifth Avenue.

Kasinec set as one of his goals the identification, consolidation, preservation, and physical conservation of those nationally- and in some cases internationally-distinguished Slavic, Baltic, and East European-related collections within the library. Before 1984, for example, original photo albums of the nineteenth and early twentieth centuries were scattered by subject throughout the division's stack area, and the Library Annex on the far west side of Manhattan. One of the first projects undertaken was the identification, checklisting, relocation, and recataloging of such items. Today, more than 5,000 original photographs are kept together in a secure area, and were very recently digitized.

Since 1984, the division has viewed its role as a disseminator of collections, not just as a repository. This has taken the form of checklists, catalogs, pamphlets, articles, and other literature describing important components of the collection. As many of the rarest items in the NYPL's holdings are dispersed among many curatorial and public service units, such compilations are useful tools for readers and staff alike, aiding researchers to understand and appreciate better the richness of NYPL's holdings.

The 1980s and early 1990s were a period of considerable federal investment in large-scale microfilming projects. The division successfully applied for and obtained four major preservation, conservation, and collection enhancement grants through the National Endowment for the Humanities and Title II-C program of the U.S. Department of Education, three of which included materials produced in the emigrations. In addition, the Slavic and Baltic Division (as the Slavonic Division was renamed in the late 1980s) succeeded in including an enormous quantity of Central and Eastern European émigré titles in the huge multi-year U.S. Newspapers Project, creating microfilm copies of many complete titles.

Collection budgets expanded during the 1980s and 1990s as well. The division was particularly successful not only in working with the administration to use endowed funds outside the Slavic and Baltic Division's allotment for more expensive items, but also in suggesting such purchases to other curatorial units—most notably, the Map Division, the Arents Collection, the Manuscripts Division, and the Spencer Collection. Perhaps the best-known collection relevant to the emigrations was the 1988 purchase of the library and extensive archives of Vladimir Nabokov, housed in the NYPL's Berg Collection.[13] However, many smaller collections of an archival or ephemeral nature made their way to the library as well, among them the Yarosh Book and Manuscript Collection, which included autographs of many notable nineteenth-century figures, including a letter from Karamzin to one of his estate managers; and a postcard from Chekhov on the topic of influenza; the Brozek Collection, which included Bohemian imprints from the seventeenth century; the Batkin Archive on the Russian Revolution and Civil War, including a diary, and ephemeral publications; the Shereghy Collection of old Church Slavic imprints; the Winters Collection of Czech and Slovak imprints; the Polchaninov Collection of displaced-persons'-camp publications; and the book and archival collection of the Rev. Dr. John Shintay relating to Slovak émigré life, circa 1880-1990.[14]

FOURTH PERIOD: 1991-PRESENT

Not long ago, the staff of the Slavic and Baltic Division attended the funeral of a colleague of the post-war generation, a proud Estonian-born and -educated patriot. The ceremony was marked by crepe-draped Estonian flags clutched by octogenarians wearing sashes and singing the songs of their university *Brüderschaft*. This moving ceremony was in many respects a metaphor for the passing of the kind of learned, cohesive, tradition-bound émigré communities that founded the division and, to a large extent, peopled its reading room for much of the past century. Today, such readers are few and becoming fewer on a daily basis. This is not to say that there are no comparable émigré communities, or that they are not reading–quite the opposite is true. However, a number of factors are affecting NYPL's émigré readership. The first is geographic. The foreign language collections of the independent Brooklyn and Queens Borough Public Library systems–boroughs with large émigré populations from Eastern Europe and the former Soviet Union–are bustling, their shelves well-stocked with Slavic and East European-language materials. The Queens Borough's International Resource Center, for example, is a state-of-the-art facility providing current materials to a remarkably diverse population. The émigré reader of today is less likely to travel to midtown Manhattan to satisfy reading needs or interests. The gentrification of large tracts of the island of Manhattan, from Harlem to the Bowery, has forced new arrivals to establish enclaves in the "outerboroughs," so there are no longer large numbers of "local" readers. The second major group of factors affecting usage by the Slavic and Baltic ethnic community is socio-economic, political, and experiential in nature. The reading tastes and habits of recent arrivals tend to be more popular, more practical–closer in many ways to those common in mainstream American society. Whereas the research interests and reading passions of previous generations of immigrants centered on the histories, politics, arts, and literatures of the homelands and families they left behind, often under traumatic circumstances, the newer arrivals know that they can always go back, and many do so frequently.

The national decline in student populations and academic positions in the Slavic and East European field, an aging faculty, and a dearth of governmental support for scholarly research are all factors affecting readership and too well known to recapitulate here. Over the past decade, the traditional backbone client constituencies of research-oriented institutions have declined precipitously. The need to amass research materials on all aspects of Eastern Europe's past and present in an era of easier access to these countries is rightly questioned by library administrators nationwide. The opening of archives in Eastern Europe has shifted the focus of academic research away from print-based sources on once-taboo research topics, toward manuscript, archival, and artifactual collections in the countries themselves. The development of electronic resources such as JSTOR and various online aggregations of Russian newspapers have called into question the maintenance of parallel print-based subscriptions. In the post-9/11 world, with economies in decline and endowment incomes depressed, such collection-building is broadly considered a luxury we can no longer afford.

Fortunately, the Slavic and Baltic Division anticipated some of these changes and began a reexamination of what we do and for whom long before the demise of the Warsaw Pact. One of Edward Kasinec's first concerns on becoming the Division's Chief Librarian was to place the collections' finances on a firmer foundation. Fundraising has been one of the most significant achievements of the past eighteen years. Since the late 1980s, individuals and organizations with ties to New York's émigré community have established endowments for Belarusian, Czech, Latvian, Polish, Russian, and Slovak language materials, helping to sustain acquisitions during good times and bad. The commitment represented by such endowments has, in turn, helped to inspire donations of private and institutional collections of research material.

Examples of major collections assembled by immigrants or their children, donated since the collapse of communism in Eastern Europe, include a substantial portion of the Fekula Collection, one of the greatest private collections of Slavic books and manuscripts in North America;[15] the Lehovich Collection of rare imprints and correspondence between Dimitry Lehovich and Edmund Wilson, George Balanchine, and Alexandra Tolstoy, among others; the archives and library of Ambassador Jan Papanek and his wife Betka; the library of Helmars Rudzitis, long-time publisher of Latvian monographs and serials. Alex Liberman of Condé Nast publishing gave his large collection of Russian popular prints; and, most recently, a comprehensive assemblage of the serial output of the Belarusian diaspora was given by the Kipel family. In 1994, the Library received an illuminated early fourteenth-century Novgorodian codex as a gift from the family of Metropolitan Ioann of the Ukrainian Orthodox Church in America.[16]

As readers from traditional categories have diminished, the division has cultivated new and diverse constituencies, including media, as well as professional (for instance, antiques dealers and magazine publishers), and other commercial enterprises. With few exceptions, such clienteles' information requirements are need-specific and deadline-oriented. Increasingly, they come seeking visual material. To satisfy their wants as expeditiously as possible, the division has redoubled its attention towards the creation of indexed checklists of illustrated books, with accompanying digital thumbnails of images. Such technology facilitates use of the collections by all readers, and paper-based publications and checklists provide the essential "metadata" needed to give thematic cohesion and accompanying descriptive text for the images.[17]

The recognition of these non-traditional clienteles' growing importance now drives the Slavic and Baltic Division's antiquarian purchases. Most of the major acquisitions of the past half-decade were of visual materials (rare engravings, plate books, and lithographs). Yet such materials benefit our traditional academic audience as well, making fresh and unusual items available for study.

During the Soviet period, individuals from New York's diplomatic community used the collections discretely, yet remained aloof. This aloofness has changed in recent years, and the library has become a major venue for public programs celebrating culture and the arts in the homelands and the diaspora. Recent events held in conjunction with the Lithuanian, Latvian, Czech, Slovak, Russian, and Polish communities have provided an opportunity to recognize NYPL's role in émigré life and to showcase collections through event-specific exhibitions. Work with the diplomatic community is part of a general consciousness-raising initiative, which includes participation in major exhibitions at the library and at other institutions around the country. By raising the profile of Slavic and East European collections with a broadly based, nonspecialist audience, we also demonstrate to administrators the viability and vitality of our collections and their interest to a broader public.

This brief overview has covered more than a century of symbiosis between the NYPL and New York's large and diverse immigrant populations. In their commentaries at the Bakhmeteff Anniversary Conference panel at which this text was first presented, Edward Kasinec, Marc Raeff, and other participants elaborated on their own experiences during some of the historical periods outlined here. Collectively, they underscored the point that, for much of its history, the Slavic and Baltic Division was a prominent fixture in the lives of successive immigrations. Although much has changed in recent years, the library remains committed to collecting, organizing, preserving, and promoting the printed and manuscript legacy of Slavic, Baltic and East European Americans and the homelands, past, present, and future.

NOTES

1. On the history of the Astor Library, the Lenox Library, and the formation of the NYPL's Slavic and East European holdings, see Edward Kasinec and Robert H. Davis, Jr. "Afterword: Collecting Slavica at The New York Public Library," in *Russia Engages the World, 1453-1825* (Cambridge, Mass.: Harvard University Press, 2003), 163-183. For a more detailed history of the collection, see Robert H. Davis, Jr., *Slavic, Baltic, and East European Resources at The New York Public Library: A First History and Practical Guide* (New York: The Library, with Charles Schlacks Publishing, 1994), passim.

2. The original petition is held in the Slavonic Division Records, RG7, NYPL Archives. A number of the signatories were prominent members of the émigré community. A search of *The New York Times* backfile, and published biographical dictionaries has produced a number of "hits." For example, the economist and publicist Isaak Aaronovich Gurvich (Hourwich, 1860-1913) appears in a number of *Times* arti-

cles from the 1890s and first decade of the twentieth century. See also his entry in *Russkaia intelligentsiia: avtobiografii i biobibliograficheskie dokumenty v sobranii S. A. Vengerova* (The Russian Intelligentsia: Autobiographies and Bibliographical Documents in the Collection of S. A. Vengerov) (St. Petersburg: Nauka, 2001-), vol. 1. Gurvich is especially interesting in that he was in close contact with the elder George Kennan (1845-1924), another one of the Library's readers and donors, and a representative of the Division's early non-émigré constituency. (He even named one of his five children George Kennan Hourwich!)

3. On Shub, see Marc Raeff, "Our First Reader: David Shub and His Times," *Biblion*, 3, no. 2 (Spring 1995): 109-125. Deich lived in New York from 1911-1916, during which time he edited *Novyi mir, Svobodnoe slovo*, and *Golos pravdy*. The Division holds materials he gave to the Library, inscribed with his name, the year, and "gor. Niu-Iork" (city of New York). Bukharin's work in the Library is mentioned in Leon Trotsky, *My Life: An Attempt at an Autobiography* (New York: Charles Scribner's Sons, 1930), 273.

4. *Annual Report of the Slavonic Department for the Year 1900; Annual Report of the Slavonic Department for the Year 1916*, typescripts, NYPL Archives.

5. The NYPL Archives contain a wealth of textual and photographic documentation for Branch histories. For example, there are more than eight archival boxes pertaining to the Tompkins Branch alone, with material dating back to 1905.

6. *Bulletin of the NYPL* 14, no. 2 (February 1910): 132.

7. Cited in the *Boston Advertiser*, 24 April, 1914.

8. See Edwin White Gaillard, "The Birth of a Czech Library," *Branch Library Book News* 4, no. 9 (November 1927): 123-126.

9. *Annual Report of the Slavonic Division for 1940*, typescript, NYPL Archives.

10. Melville J. Ruggles and Vaclav Mostecky, *Russian and East European Publications in the Libraries of the United States* (New York: Columbia University Press, 1960).

11. *Annual Report of the Slavonic Division for 1975/76*, typescript, NYPL Archives.

12. Dr. Koressaar died on 25 October 2002.

13. See Dmitri Nabokov, "History-to-Be: The Tale of the Nabokov Archive," *Biblion: The Bulletin of The New York Public Library* 1, no. 1 (Fall 1992): 7-36.

14. The Batkin Collection was the subject of the recent article by E. Kasinec and G. V. Mikheeva, "Kollektsiia F. Batkina v Slavianskom i Baltiiskom otdele N'iu-Iorkskoi Publichnoi biblioteki," *Istoriia bibliotek: issledovaniia, materialy, dokumenty* 4 (St. Petersburg: Rossiiskaia Natsional'naia biblioteka, 2002): 220-223. On the Yarosh Collections, see E. Kasinec and Antonia Glasse, "Kollektsiia Iarosh: Novoe postuplenie v N'iu-Iork Pablik Laibreri," *Novyi zhurnal* 187 (1992): 365-371.

15. Before the collection was dispersed, the contents were recorded in *The Paul M. Fekula Collection* (New York: The Estate, 1988).

16. The codex appeared in facsimile, with a history of its provenance and marginalia, in Panteleimon Kovaliv's *Molytovnyk-sluzhebnyk: pam'iatka XIV stolittia* (N'iu-Iork: Consistory of the Ukrainian Orthodox Church of the USA, 1960).

17. In March of 2003, the Slavic and Baltic Division was awarded a major NEH Preservation and Access Grant for the digitization of its rarest nineteenth-century folio plate books.

Columbia University Libraries' Slavic and East European Collections: A Preliminary History at 100 Years

Jared S. Ingersoll

SUMMARY. Columbia University Library began collecting Slavic and East European materials in the early years of the twentieth century, long before most universities in North America. Its collections of materials from and about the region slightly predate its academic programs on the area, but today the university and its libraries are, separately and collectively, widely considered outstanding resources advancing scholarship on the region. This article discusses the origins and development of the library's collections, acquisitions and exchanges, special projects for preservation and description, and the key personnel who shaped the collections and services. *[Article copies available for a fee from The Haworth Document Delivery Service: 1-800-HAWORTH. E-mail address: <docdelivery@haworthpress.com> Website: <http://www.HaworthPress.com> © 2003 by The Haworth Press, Inc. All rights reserved.]*

Jared S. Ingersoll, MA, MS, is Librarian for Russian, East European, and Eurasian Studies, Columbia University, 306 Lehman Library, Columbia University, 420 West 118th Street, New York, NY 10027 USA (E-mail: ingersoll@columbia.edu).

[Haworth co-indexing entry note]: "Columbia University Libraries' Slavic and East European Collections: A Preliminary History at 100 Years." Ingersoll, Jared S. Co-published simultaneously in *Slavic & East European Information Resources* (The Haworth Information Press, an imprint of The Haworth Press, Inc.) Vol. 4, No. 4, 2003, pp. 77-87; and: *Russian and East European Books and Manuscripts in the United States: Proceedings of a Conference in Honor of the Fiftieth Anniversary of the Bakhmeteff Archive of Russian and East European History and Culture* (eds: Tanya Chebotarev and Jared S. Ingersoll) The Haworth Information Press, an imprint of The Haworth Press, Inc., 2003, pp. 77-87. Single or multiple copies of this article are available for a fee from The Haworth Document Delivery Service [1-800-HAWORTH, 9:00 a.m. - 5:00 p.m. (EST). E-mail address: docdelivery@haworthpress.com].

http://www.haworthpress.com/store/product.asp?sku=J167
10.1300/J167v04n04_07

KEYWORDS. Columbia University Libraries, libraries, Slavic librarians, Slavic collections, book exchanges, Soviet Union, Russia, United States

Columbia University Libraries have long been recognized as holding one of the most significant collections anywhere of materials from and about the Russian Empire, the Soviet Union, and the countries and peoples of Eastern Europe. The focus of this paper is the general collections of the university libraries. Special collections, particularly the Bakhmeteff Archive, are well documented in other forums, and that research is not repeated here. That the history of this collection has not been written in the century since it began is curious, and this initial foray cannot pretend to provide a definitive portrait.

Normally, common wisdom and professors of librarianship advise that the development of significant collections at a university's library should reflect the existence of particular programmatic needs. Contrary to this maxim, Columbia's Slavic collection got its start slightly in advance of a well-defined program. However, as the libraries' collections and the university's academic programs are inextricably linked, a brief discussion of the origins of the Russian and East European studies program at Columbia will set the stage. The first offering of a Russian language course on Columbia's campus was in the academic year 1909, when Mr. Judah Joffe received a one-year appointment as a lecturer in Russian.[1] This proved to be a false start but did not predate by long the real beginning of Russian studies at Columbia. The scholar who is best credited with founding Columbia's Slavic studies is John Dyneley Prince. Professor Prince was a man of remarkable, even uncanny, linguistic ability. He studied the Algonquin Indian language as a child; his doctorate and early scholarly work were on Semitic languages, particularly Assyrian; and in his maturity he was renowned for his proficiency in nearly every European language including Hungarian and Turkish! Although hired into Columbia in 1902 as a professor of Semitic languages, Prince shifted his interests and formed a Department of Slavonic Languages in 1915.[2] His talents and inclinations drove him to resist calls within the university to limit the new department to Russian, and from the outset he ensured that a broad variety of the Slavic languages and literatures were taught.[3] By 1920 Prince had assembled a department that offered Russian, Polish, Czecho-Slovak, Serbo-Croat, and Comparative Slavonic.

While maintaining his academic appointment, Prince was simultaneously active in New Jersey politics. He was elected to the state assembly in 1906, served as its speaker in 1909, was elected in 1910 to the state senate, and in 1912 served as acting governor of the state. His political connections ultimately led to his spending the years of 1921-1933 away from Columbia as United States Minister first to Denmark and then to Yugoslavia. This example of a career split between academia and government service would be repeated by many of the scholars who founded Slavic and Soviet studies at Columbia.

A second remarkable figure of the early years of Slavic studies at Columbia is Geroid Tanqueray Robinson. Professor Robinson began his higher education at Stanford in 1913 but left before graduation, first for work as a journalist and then for service in the army during World War I. He settled in New York after his return from the war and began taking courses at Columbia to finish his Stanford degree. At this time he also wrote for the progressive paper *The Dial* and, soon, *The Freeman*. At *The Freeman* Robinson first began to write about Russia. Robinson continued his studies at Columbia beyond the end of his Stanford commitment. In 1925 he went to the Soviet Union for work on the dissertation that would become the classic *Rural Russia Under the Old Regime*. He received the Ph.D. in 1930 and stayed at Columbia for the remainder of his long academic career, with interruptions for periods in government service. Throughout his career, Robinson was a major supporter of the libraries' Slavic collections.

During World War II, Robinson ran the USSR Division of Research and Analysis in the Office of Strategic Services (OSS). In his work there, he oversaw dozens of specialists in all areas of Soviet studies. It was also at this time that he proposed the formation of an Institute for Russian studies at Columbia which would bring the same scholarly synergy he observed at OSS, to the university. His 1943 proposal received strong endorsement from Columbia President Nicholas Murray Butler and financial support from the Rockefeller Foundation. Thus, the Russian Institute was born in 1946 with Robinson its first director. The Russian Institute (now the Harriman Institute) was the first center of its kind in the United States that provided a broad interdisciplinary forum for scholars on the Soviet Union and for training experts on the region to meet the needs of government.

The earliest years of the libraries' Slavic collections are a matter of some mystery. Professor Clarence Manning, whom Prince recruited to Columbia's faculty in 1917, described their state before 1914 as "negligible,"[4] though there are clearly signs of at least some significant collecting activity before then. In 1903, the libraries purchased a private collection of anarchist literature, including many items in Russian, Czech, Polish, and Yiddish. A more significant body of material was received in 1905 from the Russian statesman and former Minister of Finance Sergei Iulievich Witte. Count Witte's gift is registered as containing 6 volumes [sic] and just under 1,000 pamphlets,[5] although no discrete catalog or checklist has been preserved. This is not a large beginning, but it certainly is enough to be considered an early milestone.

Close on the heels of Witte's donation, the library received a more significant gift. In 1907, Mr. Felix Warburg gave a very interesting collection of books, pamphlets, and newspapers numbering roughly 2,700 items. Again, no checklist remains but, from an examination of materials bearing bookplates recognizing the gift, the material was composed largely of materials published in Russia and Western Europe by Russian revolutionary socialist and anarchist parties. This material represents one of the most significant collections of such primary source material on Russian radical movements in the early twentieth century and particularly leading up to the Revolution of 1905. The library director's report for 1907 already recognizes the value of this material in light of the restrictions imposed on the Russian press during the revolutionary upheavals. The collection included many Russian publications that had been banned by the censors, with the print runs subsequently confiscated and destroyed. Already at this early date, the collections were noted for their excellent coverage not only of the broad spectrum of political opinion in the Russian Empire, but of social and economic conditions and the Empire's subject nationalities as well.[6]

Tantalizingly, a 1925 newspaper article in the *New York Evening Journal* celebrating the libraries' one millionth volume cites, in describing the libraries' highlights, a collection of material "procured for the library by its agents during the Russian revolution of 1905, than which there is no better in the world."[7] It is not clear whether the material referred to here and the Warburg gift are one and the same, but references to cost in the *Evening Journal* would indicate that this is indeed a second important collection of revolutionary materials.

Manuscript collections were also early entrants to Columbia's Russian and East European holdings. The first mentioned are contained in the 1911 purchase of the library of Sir Thomas Phillips. Included in the collection are the manuscript reports of the English Factory at St. Petersburg, written by William Morton Pitt around 1700. These describe not only the business of the factory itself, but also comment upon the political and economic conditions in Russian during that crucial period of her development.

A second component of the Phillips purchase was a collection of manuscript and printed documents relating to Poland and Sweden from Papal Nuncios for the Roman Curia, and a number of rare printed manifestos relating to the troubles of Poland at the time of the election of King Stanislaus in 1733.[8]

The years of World War I saw a total cessation of new materials from Russia. In 1917, the library director's report stated that "Russian and German publications have long since stopped coming, and nothing at the present time can be done about obtaining them."[9] The war's end brought nothing immediately to remedy the situation regarding Russian materials, though German acquisitions resumed in 1919 and Polish and Czech, in 1922. Only in 1923 did Columbia's library finally receive "58 pamphlets" from Russia.[10] The mention of such a small quantity seems to indicate that the interruption had been absolute.

The details of the books received from various countries in the early inter-war period are paired with similar figures for books sent to foreign institutions. This indicates either the beginnings of significant exchanges or, at least, a change in reporting to highlight them. In either case, exchange has been an important component in the development of Columbia Libraries' collections of foreign materials from at least this period and continued to be the main source for current imprints from Russia and Eastern Europe until about 1990. The earliest history of Slavic exchanges at Columbia University libraries is undocumented locally, but the library of the Bulgarian Academy of Sciences claims Columbia as its oldest exchange partner, as early as 1908![11] Thus it is clear that exchanges have been an integral part of the libraries' acquisitions of materials from the Slavic lands from the beginning.

The decades before World War II saw a continuing trickle of acquisitions from countries across the region, ranging from handfuls of volumes to the low hundreds. However, there were in this period two acquisitions significant enough to credit with launching Columbia's Russian collection into the highest ranks. In 1931, the purchase of the collection of late Russian historian Aleksandr Evgenievich Presniakov brought nearly 5,000 volumes, including 2,200 volumes of periodicals to the libraries. This collection was credited at the time with placing Columbia's collections in Russian history among the two or three most valuable in the United States. Of particular importance at the time were the *Polnoe sobranie russkikh letopisei* (Complete Collection of Russian Chronicles), of which Presniakov had been one of the chief editors, the 39-volume *Russkaia istoricheskaia biblioteka* (Russian Historical Library), a complete edition of the *Stenograficheskie otchety* (Stenographic Records) from the State Duma from 1906 to 1916, and a large number of publications of the Imperial Archeographic Commission. With the accession of Professor Presniakov's library, the director of libraries could claim proudly that Columbia had most of the important existing works on Russian history.[12]

A similarly strong collection in Russian literature came to the libraries in 1932 by a gift of the widow of Dr. Samuel Abel. This collection numbered about 3,500 volumes, ranging from Russian classical works to (then) contemporary Soviet literature as well as long runs of magazines and journals. For good measure, Abel had also collected quantities of revolutionary pamphlets to complement the earlier troves of pamphlets already mentioned.

On his death in 1971, Professor Robinson left his personal library to the university libraries. This was a particularly fine scholar's library, numbering in the low thousands of volumes, and including a very large quantity of rare and valuable pieces as well as autographed editions. Robinson also left a considerable sum of cash for Slavic and East European acquisitions that continues to produce significant revenue for the collections.

Little documentation concerning collecting activity between 1932 and the end of World War II has survived, with the exception of the numerical reports of the exchanges already mentioned. Purchases continued during this period, presumably under the direction of Professors Robinson, Manning, Moseley, and others from an active book market among the émigré community. Two dealers, in particular, were important at this time: Israel Pearlstein and H. P. Kraus.[13]

The end of the war saw a very important development confirming the place of the Slavic and East European collections within Columbia's libraries. The political environment of the time made doing research in Russia exceedingly difficult. Accordingly, Robinson recognized that access to information locally would necessarily be the most important tool for both students and advanced scholars, and for this, developing and maintaining a first rate library was an unavoidable necessity.[14] With the founding of the Russian Institute, the libraries answered this need and hired a specialist to oversee the development of the Russian collections. Thus, in 1946, Semen Akimovich Bolan became the first Russian Bibliographer at Columbia University. Mr. Bolan, according to eventual successor Karol Maichel, claimed to have only "four winters" of formal schooling before he came to the United States, where he studied on his own and developed an exceptional knowledge of Russian books, especially concerning the bibliography of the revolutionary era and movements.[15] He had further honed this knowledge working with the bookseller Mr. Kraus.[16] From an office in the inaccessible reaches of the eighth floor of Butler Library, Mr. Bolan oversaw the libraries' acquisition of Russian materials from 1946 until illness slowed him down in the early 1950s. In addition to steering collection development, Mr. Bolan was also responsible for cataloging a large quantity of materials during his years here, and his name is still to be found in the margin of the books he cataloged.

Karol Maichel was hired in 1952 and worked with Mr. Bolan until the latter's retirement a few years later. Mr. Maichel had studied at Columbia and knew the collections well. Even after the arrival of specialists such as Bolan and Maichel, Columbia faculty and other scholars' selections and recommendations continued to influence substantially the collections' growth and development. One notable human resource during Mr. Maichel's employment was the noted scholar and bibliophile Boris Ivanovich Nikolaevskii. Nikolaevskii was a frequent visitor to Columbia's library and was also close to Professors Robinson and Moseley. Nikolaevskii was well connected with the émigré community in New York and more broadly, and frequently identified collections that could or should be purchased. Often, his consultation with Moseley or Robinson would be enough to persuade the Russian Institute to purchase. At least until the late 1960s, the acquisitions budget for Slavic material originated almost completely from the institute rather than from the libraries' regular acquisitions funds.[17]

The use of non-standard and non-cash resources to fuel Slavic exchanges in the Russian Institute's early years is exemplified by an episode that was reported in *The New York Times* in 1956. The report describes a visit by Bolan to Moscow and a preliminary agreement to exchange with the Soviet government several original letters by Lenin for thousands of volumes of Russian and Soviet books and periodicals.[18] There is no trace of the exchange in Columbia's existing documentation, but the presence in the Bakhmeteff Archive of photocopies of the Lenin letters indicates a strong possibility that the exchange did occur.[19]

Within the libraries' administrative structure, the Russian Bibliographer was the head of a unit that was referred to as "Slavic Acquisitions," though from its inception it encompassed some technical processing and reference services in its responsibilities. In the early 1970s, Slavic Acquisitions staff reached ten full-time employees. At about this time, Slavic Acquisitions moved across campus from the Butler Library to its present home in the Lehman Library. Due to changing technology, economic conditions, and management priorities, the Slavic Acquisitions unit was reduced in 1972 from ten to six employees. The employees and their functions were transferred to other units in the libraries, so this seems to have been an attempt to centralize services rather than to downgrade the Slavic collections within the libraries. Mrs. Lencek wrote a report detailing, perceptively and at great length, many problems with dispersing Slavic acquisitions functions to many units within the libraries, but the separate existence of Slavic Acquisitions was mostly ended at this point.[20] (The location in different buildings of the bibliographer and the acquisitions, exchanges, and other technical processing units is still inconvenient. Before the adoption of the online catalog and e-mail, it would certainly have been an even greater liability.) Unfortunately, it is from this point that the documentary trail subsides from a modest flow to a trickle.

The inclusion in the early Russian collections of material on the Russian Empire's minority nationalities has already been briefly mentioned. Despite this breadth, a graduate student and later professor in Central Asian studies, Edward Allworth, discovered in the late 1950s that there was only a single book in Uzbek in all of Columbia's collections. From this revelation came the impetus to create what is today the largest collection abroad of the minority languages of the former Soviet Union. The Soviet Nationalities Collection (now, for lack of an appropriately post-colonial term, the name is prefixed with the modifier "Post-") contains approximately 21,500 volumes in 60 languages.[21] The publication of Professor Allworth's landmark *Central Asia: A Century of Russian Rule* (1967) was a major spur to the collection. The bibliographer at the time, Mr. Karlowich, sent copies to all of the academies of science as well as the republican and university libraries in Soviet Central Asia. The receiving libraries greeted this gift with a flood of publications in return and very many long-lasting exchange agreements arose from this initiative. Trips to the region by bibliographers Karlowich in the 1960s and Nina Lencek in the 1970s made libraries in the region aware of Columbia's interest in materials from the region and cultivated the personal relationships to sustain trust and productive exchanges.

A collection as linguistically diverse as the Soviet Nationalities Collection (SNC) poses obvious challenges from a technical processing angle, and for much of its history the SNC was poorly described. In the mid-1980s, thanks to a Title II-C grant from the U.S. Department of Education, the collection finally received full bibliographic description and name authority was introduced for the first time. This represents a tremendous boost for access to this material, often unique in Western collections, by researchers at Columbia and around the world. The name authority records created then are still in use, so the value of the project endures and benefits libraries beyond Columbia. As the collection continues to grow, cataloging is keeping pace, so the interested community of researchers, at Columbia and around the world, continues to have the best possible access to this often extremely rare material.[22]

Over many decades, by purchase, exchange and gift, Columbia acquired a truly vast collection of newspapers from the former Soviet Union and Eastern Europe. Columbia still holds the print editions of several thousand titles and several hundred thousand issues from the late nineteenth century through the present and from every country and region: from St. Petersburg to Leningrad and back to St. Petersburg; from Almaty to Zagreb. The resource is a gold mine for the very patient researcher, and the patience required is extreme. Most of the collection now rests in the bottom of the Lehman library, and it is in some jeopardy due, in part, to its sheer unwieldy bulk, but also to the more predictable effects of age and the occasional predations of the pathologically acquisitive researcher.

The newspaper collection suffered an encounter with such a predator in the early 1990s. A certain Mr. Nekrasov was working with the newspaper collection very intently and Mr. Beshenkovsky, the Slavic Librarian at the time, gave him detailed lists of the holdings to assist in his research. Over the course of many evenings Mr. Nekrasov hid himself in the Library after closing time, and made off with thousands of rare and valuable items, mostly newspapers and journals of the Russian Civil War and the Russian emigration. The theft was discovered soon after, and Mr. Nekrasov convicted, but a significant part of the material was never recovered. The recovered remnant is now housed in the Rare Books and Manuscript Library on the sixth floor of Butler Library.[23]

The necessity of maintaining closer physical control, as this episode so dramatically demonstrates, is a constant concern in any library. However, this is not the only danger, as time and wear pose more insidious threats to the volumes. Frustratingly, Columbia's Slavic collection is in many ways the victim of its own success: because the university has been for a very long time an established center for Slavic studies, its library collections in this field have been used intensively for decades. Such prolonged use of aging and embrittled materials has contributed to damage, thereby much unique and exceptionally valuable material is in jeopardy of being lost to future scholarship. To maintain the priceless information that has been accumulated in the past century, Columbia has made the preservation of its Slavic collections a very high priority. In the 1980s, a large quantity of newspapers was microfilmed to form the basis of Research Publications' *Russian Newspapers of the Revolutionary Era*. This collection has been a mainstay for scholars of the Russian revolutionary period. Additionally, Columbia University Libraries has received three awards from the National Endowment for the Humanities since 1992 for the preservation of Slavic materials, and so far has preserved on microfilm roughly 14,000 volumes from our collections.[24]

However, even this significant effort to preserve and make these materials available for scholarship is not enough. New technologies, particularly the Internet and digital representations of documents, demonstrate both current possibilities and future promise for making information more widely available than it has been in the past. Digital libraries of essential documents can be made available to different institutions, thus enriching the resource base all over the world. Naturally, if Columbia University Libraries and the New York Public Library (NYPL) were able to cooperate in organizing this conference, we can certainly hope to expand this cooperation into the realm of creating digital collections, reference tools, public catalogs, and more. A recently proposed Columbia University–NYPL online union catalog of Slavic serials is a first step on this path.

The presence so near at hand of the very rich resources of the NYPL Slavic and Baltic Division makes cooperation a natural goal. Indeed, Columbia's library director noted in 1911, the year that the NYPL opened its handsome new building on Fifth Avenue, that the opportunity for cooperation was very promising.[25] The traces over the years of specific cooperative efforts are hard to identify. Again, there is little documentation. The concrete traces are occasionally visible in the card catalog, where serial titles are listed as discontinued and available at NYPL. More recently, larger formal cooperative structures have played a focusing role coordinating major acquisitions. In particular, through the East Coast Consortium of Slavic Collections,[26] member universities have been able to avoid duplicating, to some extent, particularly expensive materials and to arrange for advantageous pricing for several collections.

* * *

East European and Slavic collections at Columbia University got their start quite early among American university libraries. The collections that have been assembled here are the product of a century of work by generations of specialists in the university and the libraries gathering, organizing, and providing access. All of this was made possible by a long-term commitment at Columbia to the study of the region and its peoples in all their social, cultural and political complexities. The second century promises great challenges in developing, maintaining and preserving the collection, and the Columbia University and the libraries are committed to meeting them.

NOTES

1. Clarence A. Manning, *A History of Slavic Studies in the United States* (Milwaukee: Marquette University Press, 1957), 30.

2. Clarence A. Manning, "Slavonic Studies in the United States," *The Modern Language Journal* 13, no. 4 (January 1929), 283.

3. Manning, "Slavonic Studies in the United States," 284.

4. Manning, *A History of Slavic Studies in the United States*, 56.

5. "Report of the Librarian for the Academic Year ending June 30, 1906," 246, *Librarian's Report*, Columbiana Library. Issues of a number of important serials seem to have been included in the count of pamphlets.

6. "Report of the Librarian for the Academic Year ending June 30, 1907," 192, *Librarian's Report*, Columbiana Library.

7. "Columbia has largest book collection," *New York Evening Journal*, 20 April 1925, Columbiana Library.

8. "Report of the Librarian for the Academic Year Ending June 30, 1911," 253, *Librarian's Report*, Columbiana Library.

9. "Report of the Librarian for the Academic Year Ending June 30, 1917," 332, *Librarian's Report*, Columbiana Library.

10. "Report of the Acting Librarian for the Academic Year Ending June 30, 1923," 371, *Librarian's Report*, Columbiana Library.

11. Nina Lencek, "Report on a Trip to Eastern Europe, May-June 1969," Russian, East European and Eurasian Collections, Records of the Division of the Libraries, University Archive, Columbiana Library.

12. "Report of the Librarian for the Academic Year Ending June 30, 1931," 18, *Librarian's Report*, Columbiana Library.

13. Robert A. Karlowich, interview by the author, 8 October 2001.

14. L. Gray Cowan and Geroid T. Robinson, *History of the Russian Institute, Columbia University, 1946-1953* (New York: Columbia University Press, 1954), 61.

15. Karol Maichel, interview by the author, 7 October 2001.

16. Eugene Beshenkovsky, interview by the author, 14 September 2001.

17. Karol Maichel, interview by the author, 7 October 2001; Robert Karlowich, interview by the author, 8 October 2001. Also note Gray and Robinson's report that the Russian Institute invested heavily in the libraries' collections, *History*, 61.

18. "Columbia Makes Soviet Book Deal," *The New York Times*, 7 June 1956.

19. For a fuller description of this transaction, see Patricia Kennedy Grimsted's article "Russian Attitudes Towards Archival Rossica Abroad: Cultural Reintegration or Political Agenda?"in this volume.

20. "Report on Slavic Acquisitions at Columbia University Libraries," 26 September 1973, Russian, East European and Eurasian Collections, Records of the Division of the Libraries, University Archive, Columbiana Library.

21. For a listing of the languages of the collection and holdings, see the Post-Soviet Nationalities Collection web page: http://www.columbia.edu/cu/lweb/indiv/slavic/nationalities.html (16 June 2003).

22. For a description of the grant project and the collection in the mid-1980s, see Susan Cook Summer, "The Soviet Nationalities Collection at Columbia University," *Slavic Review* 46, no. 2 (Summer 1987), 292-293.

23. Eugene Beshenkovsky, interview by the author, 14 September 2001.

24. The third award, announced on 27 March 2003, will microfilm another 7,000 volumes.

25. "Report of the Director of the Library for the Academic Year Ending June 30, 1911."

26. Members of the consortium are: Columbia, Cornell, Dartmouth, Duke, Harvard, NYPL, New York University, the University of North Carolina, and Yale.

The Hoover Institution's
Polish Émigré Collections
and the Polish State Archives

Maciej Siekierski

SUMMARY. The Hoover Institution Archives' extensive holdings of Polish material began in earnest at the close of World War II, with the deposit of several large personal, military, and diplomatic collections. Most significant were the files of the London-based Polish government in exile. These collections were followed by many others, under the direction of several prominent Poles. Agreements with the Polish State Archive since the fall of communism have provided for the exchange of microfilms of important collections. *[Article copies available for a fee from The Haworth Document Delivery Service: 1-800-HAWORTH. E-mail address: <docdelivery@haworthpress.com> Website: <http://www.HaworthPress.com> © 2003 by The Haworth Press, Inc. All rights reserved.]*

KEYWORDS. Hoover Institution on War, Peace and Revolution, archives, Poland, Polish immigrants, Polish émigrés, Stanford University, United States

Maciej Siekierski, PhD, is Curator of the East European Collection, Hoover Institution. Address correspondence to the author at: Hoover Institution, Stanford University, Stanford, CA 94305-6011 USA (E-mail: siekierski@hoover.stanford.edu).

[Haworth co-indexing entry note]: "The Hoover Institution's Polish Émigré Collections and the Polish State Archives." Siekierski, Maciej. Co-published simultaneously in *Slavic & East European Information Resources* (The Haworth Information Press, an imprint of The Haworth Press, Inc.) Vol. 4, No. 4, 2003, pp. 89-94; and: *Russian and East European Books and Manuscripts in the United States: Proceedings of a Conference in Honor of the Fiftieth Anniversary of the Bakhmeteff Archive of Russian and East European History and Culture* (eds: Tanya Chebotarev and Jared S. Ingersoll) The Haworth Information Press, an imprint of The Haworth Press, Inc., 2003, pp. 89-94. Single or multiple copies of this article are available for a fee from The Haworth Document Delivery Service [1-800-HAWORTH, 9:00 a.m. - 5:00 p.m. (EST). E-mail address: docdelivery@haworthpress.com].

Among the many unique national collections in the Hoover Institution Archives, that pertaining to Poland is one of the largest and most comprehensive. Our founder, Herbert Hoover, had a special sympathetic interest in Poland, going back to his days as a student at Stanford University, when he personally met Ignacy Paderewski, world famous pianist and future prime minister of Poland. The Hoover Institution's first Polish materials came as a result of collecting efforts during the Paris Peace Conference of 1919. In the years that followed, contacts were established in Poland by persons connected with the American Relief Administration, which Herbert Hoover directed, and which provided over half a billion meals to the hungry of Poland–literally saving the lives of many thousands of Polish children.

Though systematic collecting of Polish library and archival materials dates back to the inter-war period, it was not until the end of World War II that the Hoover Institution dramatically expanded its Polish holdings. Poland, obviously, was an important participant in World War II. The war started in Poland with a coordinated Nazi and Soviet invasion of that country in September 1939. The Polish government and some of its archives were evacuated via Romania. A government in exile was set up first in France and then in London. By 1944, that government had an army of over 200,000 soldiers, made up of Polish refugees in Western Europe as well as prisoners and deportees released from the Soviet Union during 1942. That army, commanded by General Władysław Anders, fought with distinction on the Allied side. Nevertheless, as a consequence of the agreements reached at Yalta in July 1945, the United States and Great Britain abandoned their Polish ally, withdrawing recognition from the London-based Polish government in exile. To protect the archives from dispersion or from falling into the hands of the Soviet-dominated government in Warsaw, Polish political and military authorities in the West decided to transfer some of the collections under their control to a safe location in the United States. The choice of the Hoover Institution was not accidental. Its founder, President Herbert Hoover, was respected and admired by free Poles because of his criticism of the Teheran, Yalta, and Potsdam conferences' provisions on Poland. The Hoover Library was headed from 1944 by Professor Harold H. Fisher (1890-1975), a specialist on Eastern Europe and former American Relief Administration official in Poland, an author of a major book on Poland's struggle for independence and reconstruction after the Great War.[1] In its efforts to gather Polish materials, the Hoover Institution was able to enlist the services of several prominent Poles, men such as Jan Karski (1914-2000) and Józef Garliński (1913-), as "special acquisition agents." Their work was continued during the next years by Witold Sworakowski (1903-1979), the Hoover Institution's first Curator of the Polish Collection, and later Assistant Director. The list of other Poles employed by the Hoover Institution in the years following World War II included the preeminent émigré bibliographer Jan Kowalik (1910-2001); the legal scholar and historian Wiktor Sukiennicki (1901-1982); and prewar Poland's leading expert on the Soviet Union, Ryszard Wraga (i.e., Jerzy Niezbrzycki, 1902-1968). Besides friendly administration and expert staff, the Hoover War Library was a private institution geographically very distant from the European theatre, relatively safe from political pressures and challenges. These considerations determined the decision of the Polish government in exile to move most of its archives to Stanford University.

Most of the Polish library and archival collections that were brought to the Hoover Institution in the immediate aftermath of World War II came as part of three deposits: Ambassador Jan Ciechanowski's in 1945, General Władysław Anders's in 1946, and Foreign Minister Aleksander Zawisza's in 1959. The Ciechanowski deposit included the archives of several Polish embassies including those in Washington, London, and Moscow-Kuibyshev. The Anders materials, shipped to Hoover from Rome and Cairo during 1946-1947, included the archives of the Documents' Bureau of the Second Polish Corps and a large file of materials on the organization of the Polish Army in the Soviet Union and in the Near East. The Zawisza deposit comprised the archives of the Polish Ministry of Information and Documentation as well as those of the Ministry of Foreign Affairs, which until 1959 were stored in Dublin, Ireland. The three deposits, now fully integrated into the holdings of the Hoover Institution, include rich materials on Poland's foreign relations in the interwar period and the Polish diplomatic and military effort during World War II.

However, the Polish materials are of particular value for the study of Polish-Soviet relations during that period, since they contain the fullest available documentation on the tragic fate of many hundreds of thousands of Polish citizens–prisoners of war, labor camp inmates, and deportees. That documentation is contained in the original depositions of Polish soldiers and civilians, former prisoners and deportees, about 115,000 of whom were evacuated from Soviet territory to Iran during 1942. In all, over 30,000 of these documents in various formats, and over 12,000 original release certificates from prison camps are in the files of the Władysław Anders Collection, in the Polish Embassy in the Soviet Union Collection, and in the Ministry of Information and Documentation Collection. These materials are undoubtedly the most extensive original documentation on the Soviet Gulag system available outside of Russia.

The three deposits were based on legal contracts between the Hoover Institution and private individuals. Each contract stipulated that the archives in question were to be closed for about twenty years, during which time the archives could be withdrawn from the Hoover Institution should Poland regain its independence; the archives were to become the property of the Hoover Institution should Poland remain a Soviet dependency after the expiration of the term of the deposit. The terms expired many years before the collapse of the Soviet empire over a decade ago. Accordingly, these Polish government collections are now fully integrated into the holdings of the Hoover Institution.

The great East European revolution that began with the Solidarity movement, culminating in early 1989 with the Polish Round Table, created new opportunities for the expansion of the Hoover collecting effort in Poland. Indeed, during the early 1990s, the Hoover Institution located its East European acquisitions office in Warsaw. I directed that office. This office made an effort to establish a good working relationship with the Polish State Archives. In 1990 an agreement was signed on archival cooperation with the Polish Foreign Ministry. This was followed by agreements with the successive directors-general of the Polish State Archives; in 1992 with Professor Marian Wojciechowski and in 1994 with Prof. Jerzy Skowronek. These agreements were signed despite the Polish side's position that documents created by Polish government institutions remain the property of the Polish government and that the contracts between the Hoover Institution and Polish émigré authorities were not valid. The Hoover Institution, of course, has not accepted this argument. Polish archival collections came to Hoover as a result of a carefully calculated decision of Free Polish authorities, not as the result of conquest, as was the case with Polish government archives taken over by Hitler's Germany and Stalin's Russia. The contracts were legal, they were not challenged by anyone in Poland or in the West for nearly fifty years, and undoubtedly, they helped to preserve vital historic documentation.

Both sides have essentially agreed to disagree on this basic point and to cooperate "in making accessible scholarly resources regarding the history of Poland during the twentieth century." The main point of the 1994 agreement was Hoover Institution's promise "in principle to provide one positive microfilm copy of the records of Polish government agencies that it holds to the Polish State Archives, free of charge, contingent on obtaining the necessary funding." A provision was also made for exchanging microfilms of other, non-governmental records, and for a variety of other cooperative projects.

The Hoover Institution hosted a number of visits by representatives of the Polish State Archives. A visit of several months, sponsored by the Kościuszko Foundation, to Stanford University by Dr. Władysław Stepniak resulted in the publication by the Polish State Archives of a guide to the Polish collections of the Hoover Institution.[2] At the end of 1997 the Institute received funding from the National Endowment for the Humanities and the Taube Family Foundation for increasing the level of organization and microfilming of seven of our major World War II-era Polish collections. These were the Ministry of Foreign Affairs, the Ministry of Information and Documentation, the embassies in Washington, London, and Moscow-Kuibyshev, the General Władysław Anders Collection, and Prime Minister Stanisław Mikołajczyk's papers. These seven collections represent the bulk of Hoover's Polish holdings. The microfilms resulting from this project were donated to Poland, where they complemented portions of the Foreign Ministry, of the Ministry of Information, and of the three embassies' archives preserved in the Polish State Archives. Additionally, as a good-will gesture, and with its own resources, the Hoover Institution provided the Polish State Archives with microfilms of the archives of eleven additional Polish diplomatic representations in pre-1945 Europe: the Polish embassy in Italy; consulates general in Lille and in Dublin; legations in Hungary, Denmark, Switzerland, Italy, Netherlands, Romania, and Belgium; and the delegation to the League of Nations.

Altogether, the Hoover Institution has provided the Polish State Archives with eighteen microfilmed collections, mostly from the period of World War II, totaling some 1.5 million pages of documents. Hoover Institution's own contribution to the microfilming project exceeded $300,000. As part of the exchange program, the Hoover Institution has received from the Polish State Archives microfilms of some key portions of the former Polish United Workers' Party Central Committee Archives. More microfilms have been ordered. In a separate project, the Hoover Institution has provided the Polish State Archives with financial assistance ($120,000 over five years) to process Polish audiotapes and program scripts of Radio Free Europe, the archives of which are now being transferred from Prague to Stanford University. The Polish State Archives already have copies of these tapes and scripts.

The record of Hoover-Polish State Archives relations during the past decade proves that cooperation in preserving and making historical records accessible is possible–in spite of substantial repatriation issues which even now remain unresolved.

NOTES

1. Harold H. Fisher, *America and the New Poland* (New York: MacMillan, 1928).
2. *Archiwalia polskie w zbiorach Instytutu Hoovera Uniwersytetu Stanforda* (Polish Archival Material in the Collections of the Hoover Institution of Stanford University) (Warszawa: Naczelna Dyrekcja Archiwów Państwowych, 1997).

ADDENDUM

Microfilms of Polish Collections Given to the Polish State Archives
by the Hoover Institution Between May 1999 and March 2001

1. Ministry of Foreign Affairs (1919-1947)   544 reels

2. Władysław Anders Collection (1939-1946)   131

3. Polish Embassy in the United States (1918-1956)   139

4. Polish Embassy in Great Britain (1918-1945)   163

5. Ministry of Information and Documentation (1939-1945)   279

6. Stanisław Mikołajczyk Papers (1899-1966)   234

7. Polish Embassy in the Soviet Union (1941-1944)   81

8. Polish Consulate General in Lille (1926-1940)   13

9. Polish Legation with the Czechoslovak

   Government-in-Exile in London (1941-1945)   17

10. Polish Consulate General in Dublin (1921-1957)   27

11. Polish Legation in Hungary (1930-1939)   1

12. Polish Legation in Denmark (1919-1937)   1

13. Polish Legation in Switzerland (1919-1930)   1

14. Polish Embassy in Italy (1938)   1

15. Polish Legation in the Netherlands (1920-1940)   1

16. Polish Delegation to the League of Nations (1933-1939)   1

17. Polish Legation in Romania (1919-1939)   3

18. Polish Legation in Belgium (1933-1940)   1

Total reels of microfilm: 1,599

(approximately 1.5 million pages)

Russian Archives Online:
Present Status and Future Prospects

Robert H. Scott

SUMMARY. Digitization of archival materials and finding aids can potentially become a powerful tool to provide information about and access to archival collections. This paper discusses the status of digitization of archival materials generally and applies this to the specific case of Russian materials. Digitization can offer benefits for both researcher and archivist, by making documents or finding aids available online, limiting the need to travel or handle delicate papers. However, it is an expensive process and much work needs to be done to ensure protection of intellectual property rights. *[Article copies available for a fee from The Haworth Document Delivery Service: 1-800-HAWORTH. E-mail address: <docdelivery@haworthpress.com> Website: <http://www.HaworthPress.com> © 2003 by The Haworth Press, Inc. All rights reserved.]*

KEYWORDS. Archives, digitization, electronic resources, Soviet Union, Russian Federation

Robert H. Scott, MA, MPhil, MS, is Head of the Electronic Text Service, Columbia University Libraries, 535 West 114th Street, New York, NY 10027 USA (E-mail: scottr@columbia.edu).

[Haworth co-indexing entry note]: "Russian Archives Online: Present Status and Future Prospects." Scott, Robert H. Co-published simultaneously in *Slavic & East European Information Resources* (The Haworth Information Press, an imprint of The Haworth Press, Inc.) Vol. 4, No. 4, 2003, pp. 95-106; and: *Russian and East European Books and Manuscripts in the United States: Proceedings of a Conference in Honor of the Fiftieth Anniversary of the Bakhmeteff Archive of Russian and East European History and Culture* (eds: Tanya Chebotarev and Jared S. Ingersoll) The Haworth Information Press, an imprint of The Haworth Press, Inc., 2003, pp. 95-106. Single or multiple copies of this article are available for a fee from The Haworth Document Delivery Service [1-800-HAWORTH, 9:00 a.m. - 5:00 p.m. (EST). E-mail address: docdelivery@haworthpress.com].

http://www.haworthpress.com/store/product.asp?sku=J167
© 2003 by The Haworth Press, Inc. All rights reserved.
10.1300/J167v04n04_09

This paper will discuss the status of and prospects for the digitization of Russian archival materials. Since, as I will emphasize, this is as yet a largely unrealized option, my remarks will need to wander far beyond the Russian field, but their relevance to that field will be clear.

Given the topic, it is appropriate to note that one of the first demonstrations of the potential for the digitization and electronic presentation of archival material was the Soviet archives exhibit mounted by the Library of Congress in 1992.[1] Viewers' ability in that online presentation to examine handwritten annotations and corrections of typescripts by high officials (or simply the physical form of communications between members of the Soviet leadership) was a convincing demonstration of the crucial importance of an examination not only of the artifactual document for historical understanding, but also the potential of the Internet to support such a direct examination.

Since then, there has been considerable progress in exploiting the potential of the online environment to enhance access to Russian special collections both in this country and abroad. We have seen great strides in the use of traditional cataloging to produce online descriptions of individual archival collections, particularly for those in this country–most notably, in the archival and mixed collection file of the RLIN bibliographic database;[2] in the archival files of the OCLC database;[3] and in the commercially produced *Archives USA*, which brings together the listings of the *National Union Catalog of Manuscript Collections*, once available only in print, and the guides to the American portion of Chadwyck-Healey's collection of archival finding aids, *The National Inventory of Documentary Sources.*[4] A counterpart project aimed at a comprehensive description of archival holdings in Russia itself is the *ArcheoBiblioBase* information system on archival resources, compiled by Patricia Kennedy Grimsted in collaboration with the Russian Archival Administration (Rosarkhiv).[5] This project aims to bring the same sweeping description of the field found in Grimsted's published guides to the online environment. There is also a variety of on-site and online databases and electronic guides found on the new comprehensive website for Russian archives.[6]

The varied shape, scope, character, and terms of access of archival collections have always made simple catalog records an insufficient tool for accessing their contents, particularly because an understanding of those contents is, at least in the case of more complex collections, the result of an ongoing process of discovery and description as the materials they contain are explored by researchers and curators and increasingly organized by the latter. The traditional means of capturing this information at various stages has been the local finding aids associated with a given collection, the sort of material represented in the microform holdings of *The National Inventory of Documentary Sources.* An increasing number of guides of this kind are also finding their way to the web in a variety of forms. While it is the nature of resources of this kind to vary in appearance, the similarity of issues they address has inspired the formulation of an SGML-XML standard for their electronic presentation, the Encoded Archival Description (EAD).[7] This standard is designed to support not only the online presentation of information, but also the common searching and retrieval of finding aids. The potential for the latter has found expression in *RLG's Archival Resources* database, a licensed resource that adds access to these records by a searchable interface to the more traditional collection records found in the RLIN AMC file.[8] Among American repositories of Russian archival holdings, the greatest strides in adopting this new form of online description have far and away been made by Stanford University (and the Hoover Institution in particular), followed by Berkeley and Yale. Most of the major collections in this country have accepted the notion in principle, and the prospect of its general adoption holds out the hope of a new, enhanced level of access for researchers interested in making use of those resources.[9]

Likewise, the past decade has seen the appearance of other online exhibits (or online "catalogs" and selected images from in-house exhibits), illustrating the types of materials held in larger research collections and showcasing treasures. Some, while relatively small, provide a good sense of institutional holdings in particular areas–for example, the brief but well-designed catalog of the New York Public Library Slavic and Baltic Division's Romanov exhibit[10] and the Hoover Archives' small selection of Romanov photographs from its collections[11] as well as its exhibit devoted to the American Relief Administration in Soviet Russia.[12] Others have taken a more ambitious approach–for example, Hoover's exhibit commemorating Radio Free Europe, with a brief history of the institution, a number of photographs, and several digital sound clips;[13] or its collection of 53 Russian and Soviet propaganda poster images, with accompanying Luna Image software to facilitate closer viewing and study;[14] or the Open Society Archive's extensive exhibit on the Gulag, with reproductions of photographs and documents.[15] *Russian Archives Online* takes a different approach, indicative of other issues facing Russian collections. Here the exhibit galleries of selected documentary and media images from archival repositories (primarily in Russia, although material from the Hoover Institution Archives is presented here as well) are a means of facilitating commercial use of the material.[16]

The next challenge facing Russian archives in this country and abroad, is the digitization of their content for online study and use. The online exhibit, like its hardcopy counterpart, plays a time-honored role in the life of a special collection, drawing the attention of a broader public, hopefully inspiring generous friends of the library to support further acquisitions of material, and providing a valuable education about resources and directions for research to students and scholars at all levels. However, while the exhibit can present new types of material to users, and every scholar is likely to find something of interest here, it is far less likely that the scholar will find what it is that he or she had set out to find or that more than a choice sample or two of any type of source is likely to be available. And even those materials presented are not generally adequate for full research: the images of the Soviet archives exhibit at the Library of Congress, for instance, while providing facsimiles, are generally constrained by the esthetics of the exhibit mode from presenting the entire text of longer documents. Since the exhibit is aimed at an English-speaking audience, it provides only a translation into English, rather than a transcription in the original Russian. Similarly, the images presented on many of the exhibit pages are insufficiently large to permit closer study.

Ultimately, to borrow an observation made by the Mellon Foundation's Don Waters in a recent talk on the ArtStor project, if archives are to participate fully in the revolution in scholarship made possible by the online networked environment, they need to move beyond the more traditional "greatest hits" approach to one of creating genuine online working collections of research materials.[17]

Certainly, there are a number of arguments for the full digitization of archival and manuscript materials. To begin with, technology has clearly evolved to a point where online presentation can convey a great deal of information about and support very close study of archival objects. As a case in point, consider the materials placed online by two digital projects of Columbia University Libraries, the Digital Scriptorium and the Advanced Papyrological Information System. In both cases, dense digital photography and possibilities of enlargement of the image permit the kind of close examination required to study the script of medieval and ancient manuscript hands far closer, in fact, than one might be able to examine them with the naked eye. Concomitantly, there have been developments in the standards for image metadata (amply represented in both of these resources)[18] as well as in the markup of textual content itself, the standard of the Text Encoding Initiative probably providing the most satisfactory option.[19]

Concerns about the survival of the delicate and decaying material in archival collections are certainly a powerful argument for digitization. The paper on which the vast majority of our émigré archival material is written represents the very worst of the acid-impregnated material that is so desperately at risk, and the media in which many documents are written or printed are often fading as well. Digitization provides an opportunity to capture the moment, before further loss of readability has taken place. Current digitization techniques provide an opportunity to capture colors, something not achieved by earlier microfilm approaches. Moreover, the creation of a digital surrogate, particularly when it is as effective as that described above, can sharply limit the need to handle fragile items.

In addition, thanks to the web, digital archival objects can not only obviate the need to touch fragile documents, but also the need to travel long distances to use them. Remote access means that users on another continent can access selected material, that more than one researcher at a time can examine unique items, or that archival material can be brought into the classroom at no risk. These benefits of enhanced access may provide solutions to some of the problems facing Russian collections that have been highlighted at this conference. We have heard about archives that can no longer afford facilities or open hours for examination of their holdings, about collections threatened by demands for "repatriation" of material to the homeland, and about holdings scattered by circumstance over a wide number of localities. An approach to access that is no longer dependent on physical location would seem capable of addressing many of these questions.

Preservation and access have traditionally been strong motivations for digitization projects. Arguably, the new research opportunities afforded by the online networked environment are another strong impetus. As the experience of such corpora of published texts as *Thesaurus Linguae Graecae, LION: Literature on Line*, or *Past Masters* have demonstrated, an aggregation of searchable text can support a qualitative change in scholarly research, supporting research on the occurrence and evolution of words and concepts, and the influence of one body of text upon another.[20] An online searchable database of archival holdings raises the possibility of comparing a far wider range of material than the traditional box-by-box, folder-by-folder approach imposed by current archival practice. Instead, simultaneous searching and retrieval across multiple collections or even repositories can facilitate the drawing together of related material. Rich metadata and, ideally, transcription of the content itself can support new and rapid methods of retrieval, arrangement, and analysis. The digital character of the information can potentially support types of annotation and capture of text image that would be inconceivable in a paper environment.

At the moment, aside from one international project that seeks to produce digital images and detailed metadata for their retrieval from the Comintern archive,[21] there appear to be no projects aimed at such a goal. Ironically, the most extensive digitized collection of Russian archivalia currently accessible online is to be found in the Library of Congress's "American Memory," a gathering of digitized materials on selected themes from LC's own and other institutions' special collections.[22] A search across all collections for the keywords "Russia," "Russian," or "Soviet" yields nearly 4,000 hits.[23] About one-third of that material consists of reproductions of print materials (texts from the American State Papers and other Congressional publications documenting the first century of U.S. legislative history, or nineteenth-century periodical articles from the "Making of America" project). The remainder, however, represents genuine manuscript, ephemeral, or artifactual material in digital form, concentrated in a few key collections, including documents on American relations with Russia in the papers of George Washington, Thomas Jefferson, and Abraham Lincoln; several hundred photographs of Russia in the nineteenth and twentieth centuries from the World Transportation Commission, Chicago Daily Press, Detroit Publishing Co., Office of War Information, and other sources; interview data about Russian life and customs from the WPA Life Histories project; ephemera and programs relating to Russia in an archive of Chatauqua material; and smaller but interesting sets of resources on such topics as Cossacks in Wild Bill's Wild West show, recordings of Russian Molokan religious chants, letters and diary entries about visits to and contacts with Russia in the papers of the Alexander Graham Bell family, images of Russia in works of the American variety stage, about thirty historic maps, and a handful of early film clips.

In the above roster of materials, particularly those of an archival character, non-text items predominate. Inevitably, given the need for an early return on time invested digitizing a set of objects, the higher costs involved in transcription of manuscript material, and the dominance of preservation concerns in early digital library development, the first products of most such projects have emphasized the pictorial, rather than the textual side of archival resources. Over time, however, as the art of digitizing archival materials matures, one should expect to see a growing presence of textual material in future projects, given its predominance in our archival collections. For this reason, the role of "American Memory" in retrieving items from such collections as the Washington, Jefferson, Lincoln, and Bell papers deserves special attention.

Other projects in the digital field indicate the directions that Russian archival projects might pursue. One indicator of the scale of change (though based in the field of printed books, rather than archives) is the large English literature corpus projects–*Early English Books Online, The American Periodical Series*, and *Digital Evans*,[24]–with expected continuations, produced from microform collections and providing a broad context for the study of English-speaking society. The conversion of material from microfilm to electronic format, it should be noted, has had an enormous impact on their use, particularly in the latter collections, which offer searchable full text. These projects have had their parallels in parts of Western and Central Europe, but are up to now absent (at least in professional published terms) in Russia and Eastern Europe, where literary electronic text corpus building has been largely an amateur undertaking.

The potential value of the building of such national literary corpora and the potential of earlier state-sponsored microfilming projects for such an undertaking are enormous, particularly in light of the broader context they could provide to archival study, but given the economic challenges facing most of those societies, the realization of such potential is currently rather remote. It would, therefore, behoove those of us in the West with scholarly interest in such projects to support and even promote such undertakings. More relevant, perhaps, one can point to a large number of manuscript-based projects, most frequently based on the works of a specific author–the Hartlib Papers Project, the Ibsen Corpus, or the Wittgenstein Nachlass.[25] Another interesting project of relevance to the types of documents found in our archives is Gale's database of declassified documents, featuring both images of documents and fully searchable transcriptions.[26]

Clearly, given the current state of digitization in our archives and the achievements apparent in other areas, there is considerable room for progress in our field. Indeed, there are a number of areas we could already begin addressing now. Illustrative images might easily be attached to current finding aids, giving users a sense of the kinds of materials they can expect to encounter. Likewise–and this applies primarily, but not solely, to repositories in Russia–one could make earlier *opisi* and descriptions of collections available as searchable text files, without necessarily having to worry about problems of linking to actual collection units (this was the approach, incidentally, taken by the earlier Comintern archive microfilm project).[27] Another useful step would be the presentation of representative types of Cyrillic hand online (perhaps even with the inclusion of pedagogical tools) with the aim of enabling new researchers to master the scripts with which they would otherwise have to wrestle for the first time in the archives of Russia. A similar approach might be taken to presenting the various types of official documents likely to be met with there.

There is even a basis for pursuing more ambitious digitization projects at this time. During the past few years, several repositories in this country have taken advantage of preservation grants from the National Endowment for the Humanities to microfilm some of their key collections. As the experience of such major microfilm publishers as ProQuest, Gale, and Readex has shown, the transition from microform to online digital image is relatively short and inexpensive, and the impact of such a transition on the usability of material can be very impressive. Furthermore, the experiments of those companies (as well as JSTOR) with the use of uncorrected OCR underlaying a digital image suggests that some full-text access to typescript documents may not be such a distant and unrealistic prospect.

Finally, there is much room for collaboration in digitization projects among the various Russian émigé collections in this country. Each such institution contains many individual items in separate collections (photographs, postcards, posters, pamphlets, leaflets, and other printed ephemera) that, while interesting individually, are difficult in their isolation to bring to bear in any serious way on broader research projects. The digitization of such items, accompanied with appropriate metadata, could enable them to be drawn together into virtual collections online, in which the critical mass needed for effective study could be achieved. Likewise, we have had occasion at this conference to hear of sets of papers, such as those of Prokofiev or Mandelshtam, scattered by circumstance among several archives, which might, thanks to digitization, be drawn together again for more focused study.

Lest we oversimplify the issues, an effort to address some of the potential roadblocks and obstacles is in order. For some time, certainly, the difficulties presented by the electronic Cyrillic character set in a standard ASCII or ANSI environment, particularly given the coexistence of several different systems of encoding, have been an obstacle to a more widespread online presence of Russian-language material. Doubtless this may have something to do with its relative underrepresentation on American and West European websites and with the relative slowness of the Russian field to adopt the kinds of digitization approaches described here today. Thankfully, the implementation of Cyrillic encoding by the major web browsers, as well as the ongoing progress of Unicode have helped to make this problem increasingly a thing of the past: witness the recent success in this country of such online Cyrillic information services as Integrum or East View Information Systems.[28] Moreover, by happy coincidence, the most important recent major advance in OCR technology, FineReader by ABBYY, is a software program of Russian origin, a fact that has helped to bring the creation of Cyrillic electronic text very much into the mainstream.[29]

More intractable, perhaps, are some of the psychological and institutional obstacles. Many have to do with repositories' control of their assets. If our treasures are available online, will anyone need to come to visit us again? Aside from the fact that many archival resources will simply not lend themselves to digitization and online presentation or that an examination of the original will in many cases continue to be necessary even after the study of a digital surrogate, it seems reasonable to expect that here, as in other areas of the library and information field, the online environment will increasingly affect and change the operations of archives, with an increasing amount of their interaction with patrons taking place online rather than in person. Indeed, current practice appears to involve as much remote interaction, with scholars consulting with curators before their arrival, as on-site contact.

Another source of concern is potential unauthorized use of material placed in an online setting. Online access does not necessarily equal unlicensed access. The fact that the quality of images for online display is rarely suitable for print publication, limits the attractiveness of unauthorized capture for such purposes. Moreover, tools that permit closer examination of online images do not have to support the easy capture or printing of those materials. Watermarking of images offers yet another strategy for safeguarding intellectual property rights. Such issues and approaches, whether considered separately or in concert appear to allow for a relatively secure maintenance of control of the intellectual property rights of an archival institution over its assets.

Many archives have traditionally drawn revenue from publication projects that make use of their collections, and online access may threaten this income stream. As noted, the quality of online images is far lower than that needed for print publications. What the long-term impact of growing online access to images will be on traditional image-publishing projects remains to be seen. In any case, the Russian Archives Online project (mentioned previously) appears to see this type of presentation as an opportunity to increase such sales of permissions, rather than unwanted competition with the latter.

The latter question raises a more serious one, however, and that is the cost associated with digitization. The cost of conversion to economic format involves far more than the scanning or digital photography itself. Indeed, that may be the cheapest part of the process, with higher costs associated with the cataloging, metadata, rights management, storage, and maintenance of online access. (Some recent estimates place the costs of online maintenance at as high as $140 per gigabyte of data per annum.[30]) Hence, while the topic is discomfiting for some in the academic world, I do not believe that it is unreasonable for universities and archives engaged in serious digitization programs to consider some sort of cost-recovery mechanism. Arguably, it may even be irresponsible to ignore such needs, if one is serious about continuing to provide access online to a significant body of material. Accepting the notion of cost recovery does not necessarily imply the type of unobtainably high pricing that is frequently encountered from commercial publishers of electronic resources. Models of responsible academic pricing for important resources already exist: for example, the consortial leasing models used by the Thesaurus Linguae Graecae and the ARTFL French literature database.[31]

That said, it is a rare academic institution that will be ready or able to pursue the licensing of its resources on its own. There is, moreoever, an additional argument in support of a more collaborative approach. In contrast to their counterparts in Russia, émigré archives have not been able to grow through a natural or systematic process of deposit or acquisition. Even in the best case,

their holdings reflect a good deal of serendipity, opportunity, and good for-
tune. As a result, coverage of topics is likely to be uneven, even fragmentary. A
researcher making use of Russian material in one American repository may
find relevant material in several others as well. As we begin to conceive of digital resources, particularly with a mind toward the benefits to be obtained from a
mass of searchable material, the importance of aggregating the resources of
more than one collection is immediately apparent. (Both the *Digital Scriptorium*
and the *Advanced Papyrological Information System* described above, derive
much of their authority and significance from the fact that they bring together
manuscript holdings from several U.S. and European libraries.)

Even if we could expect one of our peers to host this type of consortial activity, it is hard to imagine the model functioning effectively at this level. A con-
geries of subject special collections seeking to lease resources to one another
would represent a confused and confusing picture indeed. Instead, it seems
reasonable to expect this type of activity to take place at a higher level of interaction, at the kind of consortial level of the national bibliographic utilities that
have proven so significant for collaborative cataloging and commercial database leasing. For this reason, the Cultural Materials Initiative recently undertaken by the Research Libraries Group[32] seems worth close study as a potential
model of what we might ultimately hope to achieve in this area. RLG sets an
ambitious goal, a database bringing together "maps, photographs, objects,
documents, art, sound, and motion," in a single searchable collection, an inter-
section between library, archive, and museum. The aim seems to be to produce
on the level of the artifact, much the same kind of bibliographic control as is
currently provided at the collection level by the collection records and finding
aids in the *RLG Archival Resources* database. By providing access at this basic
level, the developers hope to encourage the discovery of hitherto "hidden collections," in part by bringing together resources from repositories that have
been unaware of one another. The database permits searching of the metadata
for the objects contained within and then provides various views of the information retrieved. The grouping is by category (subject, author, collection,
place of publication, geographical subject, personal subject, or type of resource) as a list, as a set of thumbnail images, or as individual detailed records.

Such an approach appears to work with the small set of resources currently
available (a search for "Russia* or Soviet" yields just 503 records). However,
it is difficult to imagine this approach working as effectively once the database
becomes even as large as the "American Memory" project. In addition, if this
model is to work, a metadata structure considerably more detailed than the one
being requested of current contributors is necessary. Indeed, one feature lacking
is the intermediate collection level, at least for those contributions that are parts
of collections. In this respect, the current structure of the "American Memory"

database, which supports searches across all collections and searches more appropriate to the contents of its component collections. The "Cultural Materials" database also seems less well equipped to deal with textual manuscript images than with pictorial, audio, and video material.

Whatever the shortcomings of this database, it represents the beginning of a national dialogue about the ways in which the digitized contents of our various repositories can be brought most fruitfully into contact with one another. It is a dialogue into which our Russian repositories would do well to place themselves in as timely a fashion as possible, for it will have much to do with the future shape and opportunities of our field.

NOTES

1. *Revelations from the Russian Archives* [Online]. Available: http://www.loc.gov/exhibits/archives/intro.html (20 June 2003).

2. Public access to this material is available via the Library of Congress at <http://lcweb.loc.gov/z3950/rlinamc.html>, but it is also available as part of the broader licensed database *RLG Archival Resources* <http://www.rlg.org/arr/> (both accessed 20 June 2003).

3. *A World of Information* [Online]. Available: http://www.oclc.org/worldcat/ (20 June 2003).

4. *Archives USA* [Online]. Available: http://archives.chadwyck.com/ (20 June 2003).

5. *ArcheoBiblioBase: Archives in Russia* [Online]. Available: http://www.iisg.nl/~abb/ (20 June 2003).

6. *Arkhivy Rossii* [Online]. Available: http://www.rusarchives.ru/ (20 June 2003).

7. The specification is described at the official EAD website, *Encoded Archival Description (EAD)* [Online]. Available: http://www.loc.gov/ead/ (20 June 2003).

8. Description at the official *RLG Archival Resources* website: <http://www.rlg.org/arr/> (20 June 2003). As a rough measure of the progress of the newer finding-aid oriented approach to collection access versus the older collection cataloging records, a search in that database (2/23/03) for keywords *russia? or soviet* yields citations to 6,753 individual collection records, but just 2,631 collection records.

9. A browsable and searchable set of the Hoover Institution's collection is available at <http://dynaweb.oac.cdlib.org/dynaweb/ead/hoover> (20 June 2003). A sense of the state of adoption of this form of online record can be gleaned from a search of the *RLG Archival Resources* database for the keyword "russia*" (on February 24, 2003).

10. *The Romanovs: Their Empire, Their Books: The Political, Religious, Cultural, and Social Life of Russia's Imperial House* [Online]. Available: http://www.nypl.org/research/chss/slv/exhibit/roman.html (20 June 2003).

11. *A Romanoff Album* [Online]. Available: http://www.hoover.org/hila/exhibits_prev/romanoff/romanoff.html (20 June 2003).

12. *Hoover Tower Rotunda Exhibit: The American Relief Administration in Soviet Russia* [Online]. Available: http://www-hoover.stanford.edu/hila/ara.htm (20 June 2003).

13. *Voices of Hope: The Story of Radio Free Europe and Radio Liberty* [Online]. Available: http://171.66.113.76/exhibits.php (20 June 2003).

14. *Archives–Poster Collection* [Online]. Available: http://www-hoover.stanford. edu/hila/posters.htm (20 June 2003).

15. *Forced Labor Camps: Online Exhibition, Open Society Archives* [Online]. Available: http://www.osa.ceu.hu/gulag/ (20 June 2003).

16. *Russian Archives Online* [Online]. Available: http://www.russianarchives.com/ rao/ (22 June 2003).

17. Talk at Columbia University Libraries in March 2001.

18. A good overview of the major approaches is available from IFLA at <http:// www.ifla.org/II/metadata.htm> (20 June 2003).

19. The specification, with related documentation and discussion of major implementations, is available at the TEI consortium's official website: <http://www.tei-c. org/> (20 June 2003).

20. *Thesaurus Linguae Graecae* [Online]. Available: http://www.tlg.uci.edu/ (20 June 2003); *LION: Literature Online* [Online]. Available: http://lion.chadwyck.co.uk/ (20 June 2003); *Past Masters* [Online]. Available: http://www.nlx.com/pstm/index.htm (20 June 2003).

21. A description of the project can be found at <http://www.rusarchives.ru/projects/ commintern.shtml> (20 June 2003).

22. *American Memory from the Library of Congress* [Online]. Available: http:// memory.loc.gov/ammem/amhome.html (20 June 2003).

23. 3,971 hits on 24 February 2003.

24. *Early English Books Online* [Online]. Available: http://wwwlib.umi.com/eebo (22 June 2003); *American Periodical Series* [Online]. Available: http://www.il.proquest. com/products/pt-product-APSOnline.shtml (22 June 2003); *Evans Digital Edition* [Online]. Available: http://infoweb.newsbank.com/?db=EVAN&s_start=evans (22 June 2003).

25. *Hartlib Papers Project* [Online]. Available: http://www.shef.ac.uk/~hpp/ (22 June 2003); *Henrik Ibsens Skrifter* [Online]. Available: http://www.ibsen.uio.no/his/ (22 June 2003); *Wittgenstein's Nachlass: The Bergen Electronic Edition* [Online]. Available: http://www.nlx.com/titles/titlwnac.htm (22 June 2003).

26. *Declassified Documents Reference System [U.S.]* [Online]. Available: http://www. galegroup.com/servlet/ItemDetailServlet?region=9&imprint=745&titleCode=INFO8 &type=4&id=172030 (22 June 2003).

27. See http://www.library.yale.edu/slavic/comintern.html (22 June 2003).

28. *East View Online Services* [Online]. Available: http://online.eastview.com/ descriptions/index.jsp (22 June 2003); *Informatsionnoe Agenstvo Integrum* [Online]. Available: http://www.integrum.ru/ (22 June 2003).

29. *ABBYY Software House* [Online]. Available: http://www.abbyy.com/ (22 June 2003).

30. Based on a calculation by Columbia University's Academic Information Systems in January of 2002, which takes into account the operating costs and amortization of the hardware required to maintain web files and a secure set of backups online.

31. For pricing policies of *Thesaurus Linguae Graecae,* see the reference to its website earlier in this article. Information about the ARTFL consortium can be found at http://humanities.uchicago.edu/orgs/ARTFL/ (22 June 2003).

32. *RLG Cultural Materials Initiative* website [Online]. Available: http://www.rlg. org/culturalres/ (22 June 2003).

Russian Attitudes Towards Archival Rossica Abroad: Cultural Reintegration or Political Agenda?

Patricia Kennedy Grimsted

SUMMARY. This article provokes a discussion on such important topics as the heritage of "Russia Abroad," the history and evolution of the official communist and post-communist government efforts to retrieve archival Rossica, and the importance of respecting the professional ar-

Patricia Kennedy Grimsted, PhD, is currently Fellow, Russian Research Center and Associate, Ukrainian Research Institute, Harvard University (Cambridge, MA), and the International Institute of Social History (Amsterdam).

Address correspondence to the author at: 1583 Massachussetts Avenue, Cambridge, MA 01218 USA (E-mail: grimsted@fas.harvard.edu).

The author is very grateful to the present Bakhmeteff Archive Curator, Tanya Chebotarev, and former Curator Ellen Scaruffi for assisting and verifying data with reference to the Bakhmeteff Archive holdings.

Portions of this paper were presented in Russian at the Rosarkhiv conference in Moscow "Tsel' vyiavleniia zarubezhnoi arkhivnoi Rossiki: politika ili kul'tura?" in *Zarubezhnaia arkhivnaia Rossika: itogi i perspektivy vyiavleniia i vozvrashcheniia: materialy Mezhdunarodnoi nauchno-prakticheskoi konferentsii, 16-17 noiabria 2000 g., Moskva*, ed. V. Kozlov and E. E. Novikova (Moskva: Rosarkhiv, Rossiiskoe obshchestvo istorikov-arkhivistov, 2001, 20-39). The present paper also draws on materials gathered for a larger study of the subject in preparation.

[Haworth co-indexing entry note]: "Russian Attitudes Towards Archival Rossica Abroad: Cultural Reintegration or Political Agenda?" Grimsted, Patricia Kennedy. Co-published simultaneously in *Slavic & East European Information Resources* (The Haworth Information Press, an imprint of The Haworth Press, Inc.) Vol. 4, No. 4, 2003, pp. 107-139; and: *Russian and East European Books and Manuscripts in the United States: Proceedings of a Conference in Honor of the Fiftieth Anniversary of the Bakhmeteff Archive of Russian and East European History and Culture* (eds: Tanya Chebotarev and Jared S. Ingersoll) The Haworth Information Press, an imprint of The Haworth Press, Inc., 2003, pp. 107-139. Single or multiple copies of this article are available for a fee from The Haworth Document Delivery Service [1-800-HAWORTH, 9:00 a.m. - 5:00 p.m. (EST). E-mail address: docdelivery@haworthpress.com].

10.1300/J167v04n04_10

chival distinction between "provenance" and "pertinence." It also discusses restitution issues in general and the destiny of several trophy
libraries and archives in particular. The emphasis, however, is to coordinate the efforts in description and preservation of all Russian archival
materials, whether in Russia or abroad. *[Article copies available for a fee
from The Haworth Document Delivery Service: 1-800-HAWORTH. E-mail address:
<docdelivery@haworthpress.com> Website: <http://www.HaworthPress.com> © 2003
by The Haworth Press, Inc. All rights reserved.]*

KEYWORDS. Archives, trophies of war, repatriation, Rossica, Russia,
Soviet Union, cultural treasures, exchange agreements, provenance

Since the collapse of the Soviet Union cultural circles in Russia have shown a
tremendous outpouring of interest in the heritage of "Russia Abroad." Conferences have brought together prominent figures of the diaspora in Moscow and
St. Petersburg. Recent publications include a "Golden Book" of the Russian emigration, biographical guides of émigré artists, bibliographies of Russian émigré
newspapers, and others. The highly restricted *Spetskhran* (Special Depository)
of the former Lenin Library (now the Russian State Library–RGB) has been
rebaptized the Division for Literature of Russia Abroad (ORZ). Both the
newly established Archive-Library of the Russian Cultural *Fond*[1] and the Russia Abroad Library-Fund in Moscow compete with state archives to repatriate
archival and library materials. New museums honor beloved Russian émigré
writers and cultural figures such as Marina Tsvetaeva and Nikolai Roerikh.
Unfortunately, all of the competing retrieval efforts by different repositories
are resulting in the dispersal of important émigré archives.

The Federal Archival Service of Russia (Rosarkhiv) has been in the fore-
front of an official government program to retrieve archival Rossica, drawing
considerable support from the Ministry of Foreign Affairs (MID). My collaborative work with Rosarkhiv on *ArcheoBiblioBase*, a database reference directory and bibliography of finding aids for Russian archives (http://www.iisg.nl/
~abb/), has involved me directly in these developments. Given my extensive
archival experience in the USSR and abroad, already in 1991 Russian archival
colleagues urged me to prepare a survey, analysis, and recommendations pertaining to archival Rossica.[2]

When I addressed a Rosarkhiv conference in 1993 devoted to "Locating
and Retrieving Archival Rossica Abroad," I emphasized the need to distinguish among various categories of "archival Rossica" abroad and proposed a
provisional typology. One of the bases of this typology was the importance of

respecting the professional archival distinction between "provenance" and "pertinence"–between archival materials of actual Russian provenance and those of non-Russian provenance "relating" to Russia. Within the category of materials of "Russian" provenance, I urged a critical distinction between documentation created in Russia (or the Soviet Union) and subsequently alienated, and archival materials created in emigration and hence of provenance in "Russia Abroad." I underlined, for example, the outgoing letters of Russian tsars or commissars addressed to foreign governments or those of Russian political or cultural figures addressed to foreign private recipients must necessarily and legally be recognized as the property of the receivers, even though Russian archives may understandably desire and seek copies.[3]

At a follow-up conference in November 2000, I turned to more cultural and political aspects, discussing the rationale first for Soviet and now for post-Soviet Russian efforts to retrieve or in some cases "repatriate" what has come to be called foreign "archival Rossica." Those efforts, and the term itself as now used in Russia, too often fail to recognize the typological distinctions I had proposed seven years before. The differing rationales for such retrieval in different periods has, in my opinion, not received enough attention in post-Soviet Russia.

Today an examination of this history is especially appropriate in connection with the fiftieth anniversary of the Russian Archive at Columbia University, now the Bakhmeteff Archive of Russian and East European History and Culture (Bakhmeteff Archive).[4]

ARCHIVAL ROSSICA ABROAD AND THE BAKHMETEFF ARCHIVE

I begin with several episodes from my own experience over the past forty years. Such examples will serve as an appropriate preface to my further analysis of Russian attitudes toward the retrieval of archival Rossica from abroad and toward the Bakhmeteff Archive in particular.

My first example appropriately sets the stage for a discussion of the Soviet retrieval of archival Rossica, although in this case the initiative came first from abroad. The transfer in 1956/57 by Columbia University of four autograph Lenin documents to the USSR is the only case involving transfer of original documents from the Bakhmeteff Archive. As confirmed by Columbia University, the directors of what was then officially known as the Archive of Russian History and Culture were prepared to "exchange" four original autographs of Vladimir Lenin that had been acquired as part of the Grigorii Aleksinskii collection for Soviet publications needed by researchers at Columbia's Russian Institute (now the Harriman Institute). Curator Ellen Scaruffi told me about evidence she had discovered in the late 1980s, showing active involvement in the process by Professors Philip Moseley and Geroid T. Robinson of the Russian Institute, apparently on the initiative of Columbia University Library's Russian bibliographer, Simeon J. Bolan. Those negotiations, which also involved requests for Soviet publications from the Library of Congress and the Council on Foreign Relations, took place at the height of the Cold War, when Western specialists were desperate enough to recommend the proposed exchange in order to acquire, among other items, original runs of bibliographic serials from Knizhnaia palata and reports of Party conferences. Soviet authorities at that point were quite prepared to trade such publications, and they were undoubtedly also anxious to learn more about the still closely guarded émigré archival holdings at Columbia University.

Bolan visited the Soviet Embassy in January 1956 and was excited by the alluring prospect of a visa to the Soviet Union and receiving even more Soviet publications. He gave the Soviet Embassy in advance (allegedly to expedite his visa and travel arrangements) a photocopy of some of the original Lenin autographs from the Aleksinskii collection he proposed for exchange. Understandably, the matter was kept quiet because, as Moseley explained to Bolan at the time, "if any word gets around among the exile community we are 'cooperating' in supplying any Soviet institution with unpublished materials, this can arouse a tremendous storm and can result in cutting off all further flow of exile materials to our Archive."[5]

Moseley's concern notwithstanding, Columbia's silence about the deal was not effective for long. From a *New York Times* story of May 1956 we learn that Bolan traveled to the Soviet Union that year, and brought copies of documents proposed for exchange. The *Times* highlights one of the "extremely important" Lenin letters that "contains Lenin's reaction to an incident involving his friend Roman Malinovsky, a Social Democratic Workers' Party member of the Russian Duma (Parliament) who was accused of being an *agent provocateur* for the Czarist police." In addition to the four Lenin documents, the *Times* suggests that the university would "surrender a manuscript of Mikhail Lermontov, one of Russia's great nineteenth-century poets." The Lermontov text was particularly important to a six-volume edition of Lermontov underway in the Academy of Sciences, for which it would "by coincidence . . . decide an important textual problem." Despite the *Times* report, the three original albums of Aleksandra Vereshchagin with the Lermontov text remain at Columbia University, so undoubtedly it was only photocopies that were presented to Pushkinskii dom in Leningrad. The article reports that Columbia was to receive some 15,000 Soviet publications, including issues of *Knizhnaia letopis'* and missing issues of serials, literary almanacs, and journals going back to 1802 to fill in incomplete sets at Columbia.[6] Although Columbia University has so far been unable to document that the exchange actually took place, the Bakhmeteff Archive today holds those Lenin letters only in photocopy.

Meanwhile in Moscow, already in 1958, an associate of the Central Party Archive (TsPA), Leonid Vinogradov, reported "the receipt of four original letters of V. I. Lenin from Columbia University . . . that had been sold to the university by Aleksinskii"–with a precise description of each. "Besides the Lenin documents received from Columbia University was a child's toy block, hollow inside" that had been used "to send illegal literature to Russia from abroad." Since Lenin designed it, "the block was given for exhibit to the Central Museum of V. I. Lenin."[7] Later he confirmed in print that

> . . . in September 1957 in Washington, a representative of Columbia University turned over to the Embassy of the USSR four original V. I. Lenin documents in exchange for issues of our *Knizhnaia letopis'*.

Besides the letter of V. I. Lenin to Aleksinskii, the Institute of Marxism-Leninism received letters to G. L. Shklovskii and to F. N. Samoilov, a deputy to the Fourth Duma, and a small personal memo written by Vladimir Il'ich.[8]

This and subsequent Moscow publications laud TsPA's achievement. In 1968, for example, Vinogradov recounted more details about "the visit of a representative of Columbia University in New York to the Embassy of the USSR in early 1956." He described Bolan's offer of

> several original documents of V. I. Lenin, and in confirmation gave the Embassy photocopies, . . . including the poem about the 1905 revolution. And there was also a photocopy of the same 1907 letter of V. I. Lenin that Aleksinskii had shown [a Soviet diplomat] in Paris in 1946. [9]

Unknown to Bolan, Moseley, and Magerovsky in 1956, a decade earlier in Paris in 1946 Soviet specialists had already obtained a copy of one of the three pages of the "unknown poem by Lenin" that Aleksinskii had published in the literary monthly *L'Arsh* (1946) claiming it was in the hand of Lenin. Experts of the Institute of Marx, Engels, and Lenin (IMEL, later IML), already convinced that Lenin never wrote poetry, had determined that document with verses "had no relationship whatsoever to Lenin!" They were intrigued to find that Aleksinskii had subsequently sold it to Columbia with the rest of his collection, once again "deceitfully presenting it as if it were a Lenin autograph." Bolan may have tried to include that document in the proposed exchange, but we now know that the Soviet side already knew it was a fake, which explains why that document remains in the "original" at Columbia University. As far as IMEL specialists were concerned, "Aleksinskii's deceit was fully revealed."[10]

The Soviets had also seen the autograph Lenin letter to Aleksinskii (1907) in 1946 and determined it was genuine, but they failed to obtain a copy from Aleksinskii. They were duly suspicious about Aleksinskii, who had been a leading member of the Russian Social Democratic Workers' Party (RSDRP) faction in the Second Duma, but subsequently broke with Lenin and, already "a violent enemy of Soviet rule" in 1918, went abroad. The 1956 encounter at the Soviet Embassy in Washington, DC, was apparently the Soviets' first confirmation that "Aleksinskii had sold his archive to the Americans, and again passed off the poem as a Lenin document."[11]

Actually, Soviet agents (having earlier tried to obtain the collection in Paris) thought that Aleksinskii had sold his entire collection to Columbia University, but this turned out not to have been the case. As a postscript to this episode and more characteristic of Soviet acquisition methods, it is worth noting that a decade or two later, the value of a single original Lenin letter to Grigorii Aleksinskii had greatly increased. As apparent in a letter (remaining in the Bakhmeteff Archive) to Lev Magerovsky in 1965, Aleksinskii claimed that Simeon Bolan (by then retired from Columbia) had sold "to the Kremlin" a document with some "verses in the hand of Lenin" (dated 1907), which after Soviet expert appraisal was priced at $10,000. (We know, however, the document that Aleksinskii had claimed was a poem in the hand of Lenin remains at Columbia, but the reference to Bolan raises suspicion that a more commercial transaction might have been involved with the transfer of the original Lenin letters.) Aleksinskii further recounted that Bolan proposed purchase of any remaining Leniniana Aleksinskii still had for $20,000, but Aleksinskii declined. As apparent from this 1965 letter, Aleksinskii still had some important Leniniana and was considering disposing of it. At that point he was no longer in contact with Bolan, but suggested he was disposed to discuss such matters with Moseley, if Moseley would come to Paris.[12]

Nevertheless, Soviet agents found in Paris in the 1970s what they considered an important "letter of V. I. Lenin to G. Aleksinskii of 7 February 1908," a facsimile of which had been used in a Moscow edition of Lenin's works. When, later, "the original fell into the hands of TsPA, it turned out that a major part of the document had been missing from the published version."[13] Published Soviet sources do not reveal the lengths to which Soviet agents went to obtain this letter. However, from newly opened CP archives, we learn that, indeed, the importance of obtaining the letter was so great that in early 1974 no less than the CP Central Committee Secretariat authorized an exchange whereby:

1. The Ministry of Culture of the USSR was to hand over an oil painting by the abstract artist Kandinsky to the disposition of the Committee of State Security under the Council of Ministers of the USSR (KGB pri SM SSSR).
2. The KGB will under the proposed conditions succeed in receiving the original letter of V. I. Lenin to G. A. Aleksinskii of 7 February 1908.[14]

The report does not say where the "KGB" exchange took place, but Aleksinskii had died in 1965, and the fate of the remainder of his archive and library is not clear. Columbia colleagues report that the 7 February 1908 letter had not been part of the Aleksinskii collection sold to Columbia University. Another part of Aleksinskii's collection was acquired by Harvard University in 1964, but the only alleged original Lenin letter from 1908 among the documents now in Houghton Library (only one box of manuscript materials), Harvard professor Richard Pipes considered to be a forgery.[15]

My second example comes from the early 1960s, when I was starting work on my doctoral dissertation–on Russian foreign ministers and the ideology of Russian foreign policy in the early nineteenth century. A senior colleague at the University of California recommended that I might find some materials of relevance in the Russian Archive in Columbia University. Not knowing what was held there because there was then no published survey, I tried to investigate, but never succeeded. I was informed how extremely difficult it then was to gain access to the Russian Archive. After I pursued the matter further with several elder specialists reputed to be "insiders," I was informed that there were no materials of any significance for my topic. (I later learned that this was incorrect, but in those days, I was attuned to Soviet-type archival refusals.)

A third example comes from the early 1970s. Following successful forays into Soviet archives, I was assisting with a visit by several Soviet archivists, including Gennadii Belov, Chief of the Main Archival Administration (Glavarkhiv, Rosarkhiv's predecessor). At the request of the office of the Archivist of the United States, I tried to arrange a visit for Belov to the Russian Archive at Columbia University, because colleagues at the National Archives were having difficulties. My request, too, was categorically refused. I never met Lev Magerovsky (then Curator) in person, but was told that he would not permit any Soviet representatives to visit, nor would he permit a detailed description of the archive to be available publicly. At the time, in my youthful naiveté, I was not very sympathetic to Magerovsky's position. Today not only do I sympathize, but I fully understand that his attitude was caused by some of the Soviet attitudes and procedures I will be describing.

A fourth example involves the delays in description of the Bakhmeteff Archive (as the Russian Archive at Columbia had been renamed in 1975), which was started only after Magerovsky's retirement in 1972. Indeed the first published description of the holdings was to be included in John Brown and Steven Grant's impressive compilation describing archival materials pertaining to Russia and the USSR in the United States and Canada. As a consultant to their project, I reviewed their description of the holdings of the Bakhmeteff Archive in the late 1970s.[16] I tried to get them to include reference to the new detailed card catalogs (many on the level of individual document) being created under a grant from the National Endowment for the Humanities by Steve Corrsin and his colleagues. It was too late, and it was another eight years before a collection-level guide to the Bakhmeteff Archive appeared! In the early 1980s, the newly appointed Archivist Ellen Scaruffi created RLIN (Research Library Information Network) entries for all of the collection-level descriptions, which formed the basis for the 1987 published guide.

By that time much of the card catalogue had been completed, and RLIN records were already available electronically. Yet a Soviet professor from the Moscow State Historico-Archival Institute (MGIAI), who had been given access to the archive at the beginning of the 1990s, published a report after his return to Moscow strongly criticizing the lack of finding aids in the Bakhmeteff Archive. He complained that the archive was inadequately described, because there were no Soviet-style *opisi*.[17] Apparently neither knowing English adequately nor discussing his needs with the curator, he had not understood that the card catalogue and RLIN collection-level entries for most of the holdings were readily available to researchers!

A final example comes from the early 1990s, when Bakhmeteff Curator Ellen Scaruffi described to me a letter received from Dmitrii Likhachev urging the transfer, i.e., "repatriation" of the Bakhmeteff Archive to Moscow. If it were not possible to transfer all the originals, the follow-up suggestion was for Columbia University to provide microfilm copies of everything. That, of course, was out of the question, but the request from Likhachev was not the only such plea that the Bakhmeteff Archive received. Russians simply do not understand the concept that major university or other publicly accessible repositories of archival Rossica abroad could never conceive of transferring to Russia the holdings that they have acquired, preserved, described over decades at tremendous cost and effort, and developed as part of major academic institutions.

Likhachev's queries are duly representative of, and possibly even instigated by, the official post-1991 state archival Rossica retrieval program that has a long history in Soviet and now Russian governmental circles. And such attitudes have been resurfacing recently in many post-Soviet Russian political, cultural, and academic circles, as well as the archival world.

TO LOCATE AND RETRIEVE
OR TO RESPECT FOREIGN PROVENANCE
AND PROFESSIONAL PRESERVATION ABROAD?

Changing Russian attitudes in different periods towards "archival Rossica abroad" and the motivations for its retrieval to the "home country" have had an important influence on the specific "archival Rossica" that have been retrieved, from whence and when, as well as the fate of materials from abroad now in Russia. Such attitudes also have affected the type and extent of description of those materials available to researchers. Too often both researchers and archivists in Russia do not know when, where, how, and under what circumstances particular documents and collections have been acquired.

The intellectual context of and rationale for current Russian efforts to find and retrieve archival Rossica abroad stem in part from the crisis of Russian national historical and cultural identity following the collapse of the Soviet Union. They can be seen as aspects of a new Russian nationalism and increasingly self-conscious right-wing patriotism in contrast to earlier Soviet policies, although a strong legacy of Soviet-era preoccupations persists. Since 1991, Russian intellectuals of all political persuasions have been actively seeking reintegration with Russia Abroad–the "lost" or exiled Russian history and culture in exile and/or emigration. The crowds that gathered to welcome Solzhenitsyn and Rostropovich when they returned from exile represent a broader cultural manifestation of the same phenomenon.

OFFICIAL STATE EFFORTS
FOR THE RETRIEVAL OF ARCHIVAL ROSSICA

An interview with the now-Chairman of the State Archival Service of the Russian Federation (Rosarkhiv), Vladimir Kozlov, that appeared in *Izvestiia* in 1994 reflects a broader publicistic appeal.[18] Noticeably Ella Maksimova (the journalist involved), and Kozlov himself in response, failed to distinguish between "intellectual" (i.e., descriptive) and "physical" retrieval. That article caused Elliot Mossman, then Editor of the *Slavic Review*, to express editorial alarm about Russia's new "aggressive effort to solicit and barter abroad for the dispersed Russian patrimony," implying that the new, vocal interest in foreign archival Rossica revealed a "new cultural imperialism." He even suggested it was linked to the difficulties Russian intellectuals, even those of a liberal persuasion, were having coming to terms with the "end of empire."[19]

Being closer to the Russian archival scene at the time, I initially took exception to Mossman's editorial. Mossman was unaware of the December 1993 Rosarkhiv conference, and his comments accordingly did not account for the new context in which it took place. When I related Mossman's comments to Kozlov, he vehemently denied the charges and urged me to speak out. Yet we can best understand both Mossman's editorial and Kozlov's defensive response in the light of earlier Soviet policies. Today, Rosarkhiv's purported goal, and the reason for the government's support for retrieval of archival material, is primarily cultural. At the same time, retrieval or "repatriation" has become an official state political aim. The December 1993 conference, following the official Rosarkhiv resolution of 16 December 1992–*Vyiavlenie i vozvrashchenie zarubezhnoi arkhivnoi Rossiki*–made the search for and retrieval of archival Rossica abroad a matter of state policy as well as a purely cultural phenomenon. Kozlov himself made this clear in his address to the conference.[20] The November 2000 Rosarkhiv conference followed suit seven years later and was intended to present progress reports.

The question of whether we are dealing with the retrieval of original documents or intellectual information about the foreign complex of archival Rossica was only one aspect of the problem. Equally important for the American editor, if not more so, was the right of individual Russian émigrés or their families to decide for themselves where they want their personal papers to be deposited, a right he feared was not being adequately respected by new laws in the Russian Federation. Why shouldn't Nadezhda Mandelstam, rather than the Russian State Duma or Rosarkhiv, have the right to decide whether her papers and those of her husband should reside for posterity in Moscow or in Princeton University Library?

Indeed, the 1993 Russian archival law and subsequent regulations regarding the "Archival *Fond* of the Russian Federation"–in contrast to the legal basis in many Western countries–continues a strong Soviet tradition to emphasize significant *state* proprietorship and responsibility for the entire archival heritage of the country, public as well as private. Unlike those in many foreign countries, Russian laws even prohibit the export of all "non-state" or personal papers or collections created outside of official governmental functions. Thus under current Russian law an individual writer such as Nadezhda Mandelstam or a religious community such as the Schneersohn Lubavitch Hassidic Jewish Community (now in Brooklyn) would not have the right to alienate archival materials from the country, once they are considered part of the "Archival *Fond* of the Russian Federation."[21]

ROSSICA AND RESTITUTION

Particularly noticeable today in political terms is the extent to which the search for and retrieval of "Rossica," and/or "Sovietica," abroad has been consciously and politically linked with "archival restitution" by the Russian Federation involving the massive quantities of displaced or "trophy" archives in Russia–especially those plundered by Soviet authorities in Germany and Eastern Europe in the wake of World War II. The link was blatantly stated at the 1993 Rosarkhiv conference by Igor Budnik, representative of the Ministry of Foreign Affairs and then director of the Archive of Foreign Policy of the Russian Empire (AVPRI).[22] Pressure from Western and Eastern European countries for restitution of captured records, since their existence was finally revealed in 1991, has become a special occasion for Russian political and archival leaders to barter for archival Rossica abroad in return. Russian archival leaders and politicians alike often do not even want to recognize the difference between archival materials of Russian provenance and those created abroad by exiles or émigrés, or personal papers legitimately taken abroad. While many Russian professional archivists, understanding international professional principles and precedents, are prepared to return the millions of files of foreign records held in Moscow, they face an emotional public outcry against the restitution process. The Russian Duma even used the example of the fragments of the Smolensk Party Archive that were first plundered by the Nazis from Smolensk, then removed from the U.S. restitution center at Offenbach by American Army intelligence agents, and long held in the United States, to justify non-return of foreign records held in Moscow.[23]

In point of fact, the United States did offer to return the 541 files of the "Smolensk Archive" in 1965, though this was not known publicly in Russia. At that point, Glavarkhiv Chief Gennadii Belov advised the Soviet Foreign Ministry against claiming them:

> An official petition by the Soviet Union to the State Department could be used in the USA as an official recognition of the authenticity of those documentary materials, and thus even contribute to falsified display in public exhibits and further published utilization with the aim of anti-Soviet propaganda and hence appear to substantiate concrete examples of events which took place during the 1930s.
>
> In this connection, GAU recommends that it is not appropriate at the present time to raise with the State Department the question of the return of the Smolensk Archive, and especially because it currently presents no special practical value. The Ministry of Foreign Affairs agrees in this matter.[24]

A quarter of a century later in the spring of 1992, then Archivist of the United States, Don Wilson agreed to return the so-called "Smolensk Archive" held in the U.S. National Archives. But at that point cultural restitution politics came into play on the American side as well: U.S. Senators signed a resolution using the Smolensk Archive as barter on behalf of the Schneersohn heirs in Brooklyn, who were trying to obtain the library collection from the prerevolutionary Hasidic community from Lubavichi (Smolensk Oblast') that had been nationalized by the Lenin Library after the group fled Russia in 1918. The proposed U.S. act of restitution was taken off the agenda for the June 1992 Bush/Yeltsin Summit in Washington. Later, Vice-President Gore's Office continued to press the Schneersohn cause and had a special advisor dealing with the issue.[25]

Finally on 14 December 2002, the 541 files of the "Smolensk Archive" were turned over to Russia by the U.S. State Department in Washington, DC, and by the U.S. Ambassador in Moscow in a formal ceremony at the Ministry of Culture. There was no immediate "barter" in that U.S. act of restitution, but politics continued to be involved at the highest levels with the symbolic bit of archival Rossica. The "gesture of goodwill" came as a follow-up to the State Department-sponsored 1998 Washington Conference on Holocaust-Era Assets, particularly with pressure from the Commission for Art Recovery in New York, headed by Ambassador Ronald Lauder, in connection with the agreement for a "Project on Art and Archives" signed with the Ministry of Culture in 2001. The aim was to encourage description of cultural treasures in Russia that had been the property of Holocaust victims in Western Europe.[26]

France was the first country after 1991 to retrieve some of its twice-plundered archives from Russia. After German records, archives of French provenance were most voluminous of all foreign captured records in Moscow. Barter for archival Rossica was an essential part of the process, and even the official authorizing laws of the Russian Duma used only the word "exchange" rather than "restitution" or "return." The latest restitution transfers to France took place in 2000 and 2001, but still not all the archival materials of French provenance in Moscow have been identified or returned.[27] As an archivist from the French Ministry of Foreign Affairs responded during a seminar on the subject in Paris, she was concerned that France would never see the return of all its archives from Moscow, because the French were "down to their last carrot" in terms of archival Rossica in France needed to continue the restitution process.

Barter was also involved in the 1996 Duma-approved return of archival materials to the Grand Duchy of Liechtenstein. Again, the act of restitution authorized export of Liechtenstein "family archives," which "had no bearing on the history of Russia," in "exchange" for the Sokolov collection relating to the assassination of the Russian imperial family purchased by the Liechtenstein royal family from Sotheby's. A similar exchange was involved with the return of the Rothschild family papers from Vienna following ten years of negotiations: the Russians finally handed them over to the director of the Rothschild Archive in London in exchange for a collection of over 5,000 love letters of

Russian Emperor Alexander II to his morganatic wife, Princess Ekaterina Iur'eva [Dolgorukii], purchased from Christie's by the family for the prospective "barter."[28]

An even larger-scale barter in "Rossica" was involved with the multi-million-dollar microfilming agreement with the Hoover Institution and the British microform publisher Chadwyck-Healey. As one of the conditions of the deal, the Hoover Institution was to provide Rosarkhiv with microfilm copies of all Russian-related archival materials in the Hoover archives. As portrayed in Russian press accounts, even that was not enough to satisfy the Russian public, who were up in arms against Rosarkhiv for "alienating the national patrimony" by sale of microfilming rights to the country's "paper gold."[29]

With so many achievements in the retrieval and "repatriation" of archival Rossica during the 1990s, Rosarkhiv still eyes the Bakhmeteff Archive at Columbia University. At a reception in May 2002 at the Belgian Embassy in Moscow in connection with the transfer of archives of Belgian provenance that were brought to the USSR after World War II, again the transaction was officially dubbed an "exchange." In that case, again after ten years of difficult negotiations, Rosarkhiv netted only a relatively small quantity of microfilms of documentation from a Belgian military museum. Hardly was the ink dry on the "exchange" documents when Rosarkhiv Chief Vladimir Kozlov turned to me expressing his hope that I was "satisfied" by what I had witnessed. But then he went on to inquire, "When can we expect the return of the Bakhmeteff Archive?" Taken aback by such a seemingly threatening remark, my retort was one of shock and surprise: "Certainly, I don't think there is any chance of that!" Kozlov was not easily satisfied: "We already have proof that Bakhmeteff wanted the materials returned to Russia," he continued. "I doubt our colleagues at Columbia University have ever heard about that," I suggested. Indeed, Bakhmeteff Curator Tanya Chebotarev had recently received telephone calls from the Russian Embassy in Washington regarding specific émigré collections in the Bakhmeteff Archive. After she suggested that any pretensions should be presented officially in writing so they could be thoroughly investigated, the matter cooled down and the phone calls stopped.

POSTREVOLUTIONARY SOVIETICA RETRIEVAL–
TsPA AND THE SOCIALIST COMPONENT

Generally, before the Revolution, more cosmopolitan attitudes prevailed and Russian scholars and archeographers had been content to describe and publish editions of Russian-related archival materials abroad. In the immediate postrevolutionary decades, "Rossica" per se or its description did not attract much attention. The highest priority in the 1920s and 30s in the search for the archival heritage abroad was the retrieval of what might better be labeled "Sovietica"–sources for the history of revolution and the European left-wing socialist labor movement. The rich collections of the former Central Party Archive (Tsentral'nyi partiinyi arkhiv, TsPA) attest to the success of that process.[30] The paper legacy of Vladimir I. Lenin was the most important element. The details recounted in the Soviet-published monograph by Roman Peresvetov, *Search for the Priceless Legacy,* and the TsPA annual acquisition reports demonstrate the extraordinary attention focused on retrieval of Lenin documents.[31] Other accounts of the retrieval of Leniniana reveal more examples of the successes and failures of repatriating Lenin autographs from abroad. For example, lengthy chapters in another monograph devoted to the formation of the Lenin *fond* (*fond* 2) in TsPA detail efforts from the 1920s to the 1980s.[32] In almost all such publications the Columbia transfer of the four original Lenin letters appears as a highlight. While such Communist Party publications do not mention the exchange of a Kandinsky painting for a Lenin autograph, that exchange turns out not to have been unique. A second KGB transaction for the acquisition of a letter of Karl Marx and two letters of Lenin in 1975 can also now be documented from other recently opened Communist Party files in Moscow. While again few details are yet available as to the agents or place involved, we know only that a Malevich or Kandinsky painting was given out from Moscow in the trade.[33] Allegedly there are more such examples demonstrating the high price of retrieval for Leniniana during the Soviet regime.

The process of searching for key archival materials of "anti-Bolshevik traitors" or other potential "enemies" of the Soviet regime also got started in the 1930s. The most prominent example was the seizure of some Trotsky papers from the Paris Branch of the International Institute of Social History on the night of 6 November 1936, undoubtedly by the OGPU. To be sure, these captured files were not added to the Trotsky *fond* in TsPA and undoubtedly stayed with the files of the security services, although some may today be among the Trotsky papers that have ended up in the Presidential Archive (AP RF) and remain classified in Moscow.[34]

ROSSICA RETRIEVAL IN THE 1930s– BONCH-BRUEVICH AND THE STATE LITERARY MUSEUM

Broader interest in cultural and literary archival Rossica abroad was kept alive, most particularly by Lenin's Bolshevik comrade Vladimir Bonch-Bruevich, as director of the State Literary Museum in Moscow. Bonch-Bruevich was among the most active in Russia during the 1930s in keeping tabs on archival Rossica abroad.[35] His top priority was the extensive "Russian Archive under the auspices of the Ministry of Foreign Affairs" in Prague, which he had described in a personal appeal to Stalin already in 1935.[36]

POST-WORLD WAR II ROSSICA, REPARATIONS, AND "TROPHIES OF WAR"

At the end of World War II, Bonch-Bruevich was much more aggressive in recommending retrieval, as exemplified in his February 1945 letter to Stalin. In fact, Bonch-Bruevich was the cultural imperialist of archival Rossica *par excellence*, as he identified major collections of Rossica:

> held within the aggressor countries and their satellites (i.e., Germany, Austria, Romania, Hungary, Finland, and Bulgaria) . . . Such archives should be confiscated from those countries completely and entirely–Russian manuscripts, documents, correspondence, portraits, engravings, paintings, valuable rare books from libraries, substantial specialty objects among others, and even all Slavonic manuscript books. Most important from Germany–all Russian materials, all Slavic materials, with nothing left behind.[37]

In Czechoslovakia his top priority remained the *Russkii zagranichnyi istoricheskii arkhiv* (Russian Historical Archive Abroad, RZIA). Bonch-Bruevich added the important caveat that such confiscation had as its ultimate aim "thorough study, and–even more important–quality scholarly publications." Not unlike Russian nationalists and many intellectuals today, he emphasized "the extent to which such materials are needed for our history, for our literature, and for our scholarship."[38] The Commissariat of Foreign Affairs and the NKVD archival authorities in 1945 rejected the aggressive extent of Bonch-Bruevich's recommendations. Nevertheless, the search for and retrieval of Rossica/Sovietica abroad had already begun in full swing and, at that point, neither hard currency, nor "degenerate art," nor archival documents to barter were necessary.

ROSSICA AND UCRAINICA FROM PRAGUE– THE RZIA "GIFT"

In contrast to Bonch-Bruevich, Stalin's NKVD security chief, Lavrentii Beria, and the SMERSH archival scouts were most interested in Rossica, but not because it represented "lost elements" of Russian culture. They were anxious to retrieve archival Rossica that could serve their immediate "operational" aims to identify members of various Russian émigré factions involved in "anti-Soviet" activities. The acquisition of RZIA was a case in point. A few days after *Pravda* announced the "gift of the Czech government to the Academy of Sciences of the USSR" in June 1945, the Commissariat of Internal Affairs determined that "the documentary materials in RZIA should be considered an integral part of the State Archival *Fond* of the USSR and should be returned to the Soviet Union."[39] Already in October 1945 one freight car of archival materials from the subsidiary Ukrainian Historical Cabinet (UIK) and related captured Ukrainian émigré materials were shipped to Kyiv, where unfortunately, they have still not been described and made publicly available, although Ukrainian security services quickly took them under control.[40]

Immediately after the nine sealed freight cars from Prague arrived in Moscow in January 1946, the NKVD Secretariat sent Stalin a two-page "Special File" (*Osobaia papka*) characterizing the seized documentation. The Academy of Sciences officially turned its "gift" over to the Central State Archive of the October Revolution of the USSR (TsGAOR SSSR).[41] Several months later, Deputy Commissar of Internal Affairs Sergei Kruglov assured Zhdanov that the archive would be expeditiously analyzed for "data on anti-Soviet activities of the White emigration to be used in operational work of organs of the Ministry of Internal Affairs (MVD) and Ministry of State Security (MGB) of the USSR."[42] By October, they had completed 10,000 cards from the "*fonds* of the White counter-revolutionary government and their military units," in addition "to preparing 4,560 reports (*spravki*) in answer to inquiries of operational organs."[43] Many of the cards prepared are now open to researchers in GA RF. We still do not know how many of the documents were used as a basis for arrests and incarcerations under the Communist regime. Yet we do know that at least three of the RZIA archivists and librarians who went to the USSR from Prague were imprisoned in the USSR: two of them perished in prison, a third died soon after his release.[44] Lev Magerovsky, who had been curator of émigré serials in RZIA in Prague was lucky enough to escape and come to New York. Instead of going East or remaining under persecution in Prague, he was able to continue the RZIA tradition in the United States as Curator of the Russian Archive. In contrast, most of the RZIA archival materials that went to Moscow were not available to researchers in Soviet archives until the late 1980s.[45]

During the Cold War, it is little wonder that Russian exiles and émigrés, such as Magerovsky at Columbia, refused to admit Soviet citizens, publish descriptions, or make available in public catalogs information about émigré archival holdings, for fear that Soviet authorities would attempt to pilfer the materials or use them to compromise individuals therein described. Only in 1987, a year after Magerovsky's death, was a guide to the Bakhmeteff Archive finally published. In Russia, a comprehensive inter-repository guide to the RZIA collections was published in Moscow in 1991, which helps identify the holdings that were unfortunately dispersed to approximately thirty repositories throughout the USSR.[46]

ROSSICA RETRIEVED FROM OTHER COUNTRIES

There are still examples of *fond*s (or parts thereof) listed in the new RZIA guide that did not come from RZIA, or even from Prague. The considerable archival Rossica that Soviet authorities "retrieved" from other countries of Eastern Europe has never been adequately documented in print, and its extent has been little known in Russia. Identification is now exceedingly difficult, because at the time there was no effort to preserve traces of provenance and sources of acquisition, and many files were intermixed with those from RZIA. The entire division in TsGAOR SSSR became known as the RZIA Division, but that was clearly a misnomer, because much of it did not come from Prague.

By February 1945, Soviet archival agents were already on the scene in Romania, seeking émigré collections of "operational" interest. In Bucharest they recovered the archive of an International Refuge Office that had helped refugees after the October Revolution.[47] Most important were parts of the archive of the former imperial Russian Embassy and two crates of papers from former Russian ambassador Aleksei Savinov that were among the large shipment to Moscow.[48]

From Bulgaria, archives of Herzen and Ogarev that Bonch-Bruevich had recommended were brought to Moscow as a "gift" of the Bulgarian Academy of Sciences.[49] Two years later, in May 1947, eighty-two crates of Russian émigré-related files having "serious operational and historical significance for the Soviet Union" were shipped to Moscow from Yugoslavia and dispersed to several different archives.[50] Materials from the Belgrade museum honoring Nicholas II now in the State Historical Museum (GIM) have recently been described.[51]

In Northern Manchuria a brigade of archivists (with SMERSH assistance) retrieved extensive documentation from Russian émigré communities in Asia, especially Harbin.[52]

NAZI-CONFISCATED
EUROPEAN ROSSICA/SOVIETICA FROM SILESIA:
THE REICH SECURITY MAIN OFFICE (RSHA) COLLECTIONS

The Nazi Security Main Office–RSHA (*Reichssicherheitshauptamt*) was also very interested in archival Rossica among their other archival and library loot from "enemies" of its regime, such as Jews and Masons. A Soviet trophy brigade discovered their extensive cache of archives plundered from many European countries, held in a castle in the remote Silesian village of Wölfelsdorf (now Polish Wilkanów), which included holdings from the Paris Branch of the International Institute of Social History (Amsterdam), headed by Boris Nikolaevskii. Beria personally ordered a Glavarkhiv delegation to the spot, and twenty-eight freight-cars of documents were transported to Moscow.[53] Most of the Russian émigré files from Wölfelsdorf were deposited in TsGAOR SSSR (now GA RF), where they were intermingled with the Prague materials from RZIA. Such was the fate, for example, of the papers and personal library of Pavel Miliukov that the Nazis had looted from Paris. Similarly, some of the Socialist-Revolutionary collections, such as the papers òf Viktor Chernov and Boris Nikolaevskii from Paris, were intermixed with other files of personal papers of the same individuals that had come from RZIA and then were treated as if they had all come from Prague. Some of the Communist-related materials, including individual Lenin letters, were separated out and transferred from TsGAOR SSSR and many other archives to the Central Party Archive (TsPA) in Moscow. Given such undocumented dispersal and integration, archivists today have difficulty tracing their migration.[54]

MORE EUROPEAN ROSSICA/SOVIETICA–
RATIBOR AND THE EINSATZSTAB REICHSLEITER ROSENBERG

Soviet military trophy brigades in the Kattowitz area of Silesia (now Polish Katowice) found additional archival "Rossica" looted by the Einsatzstab Reichsleiter Rosenberg (ERR) from Western Europe. From 1943 until January 1945 the main ERR research center and library reserves for their "Anti-Bolshevik" research and propaganda operations was centered in the city of Ratibor (now Polish Racibórz), about seventy kilometers southwest of Kattowitz. Soviet scouts found the Turgenev Russian Library and the Petliura Ukrainian Library, both confiscated from Paris, in warehouses near Kattowitz. Along with these libraries were other captured archival and library treasures from France and other Western European countries, as well as an estimated one million books from Belarus and the Baltic nations. In the case of the two Slavic libraries from Paris, some of the holdings went to Minsk, some to a Red Army Officers' Club in Silesia, and some to Moscow. Archival materials from the Petliura Library have ended up in two archives in Moscow and two in Kyiv, and its books have recently been identified in Moscow, Kyiv, and Minsk.[55] In the spring of 2002, the Russian State Library, after half a century of silence, finally admitted to having an estimated eight to ten thousand books from the Turgenev Library in different divisions.[56] Other books from the Turgenev Library are now dispersed from Minsk to Voronezh and the island of Sakhalin. That Paris Russian library held few archival materials before the war, but RGB has some of its own twice-plundered administrative files, and other files from its archive are now dispersed in two *fonds* in GA RF and two different files in the former Central Party Archive (now the Russian State Archive of Socio-Political History (RGASPI). In the latter case, there is even an original Lenin letter that was separated from the rest of the Turgenev Library archive for transfer to IML.[57]

ROSSICA RETRIEVED
FROM OCCUPIED GERMANY AND AUSTRIA

In terms of the "Rossica" component of the extensive postwar archival seizures by Soviet military and civilian authorities, we have noted two prime categories of targets–first, twentieth-century Russian émigré materials relating to the Civil War and foreign intervention, the White political emigration, and records of émigré communities abroad. These materials were retrieved everywhere they were found for their potential "operational" use. Second, perhaps of equal priority, were materials relating to the revolutionary socialist movement that were considered of prime "historical-scientific" value. In neither category was the distinction made as to whether or not the files involved were created within the lands of the former Russian Empire or Soviet Union and then alienated, or whether they had been created abroad in exile or emigration. All were important for the advancement of Communism under Moscow's auspices and the corollary struggle against "anti-Soviet elements" by "operational" organs.

Most of the Bolshevik-oriented Rossica component was deposited in the Central Party Archive (TsPA). As elsewhere, by the time files reached that repository, many of the details of where they had originated no longer accompanied them. When the TsPA started to open its doors to outside researchers in 1990, the LaSalle papers was the only *fond* specifically identified as having been retrieved from Germany after the war, and archival authorities initially denied the existence of any other captured records.[58] Because many of the other files deposited in TsPA have been integrated into other preexisting *fonds*, archival authorities today may well not even know from whence they came, and it will be exceedingly difficult to trace their migration. For example, the French intelligence file on Trotsky was evidently added to his *fond* in TsPA.[59] Presumably, similar French intelligence files on Stalin and other Soviet leaders have been dispersed in many other *fonds*.

Most tragically from a scholarly standpoint, the vast quantities of archival Rossica that Soviet authorities "retrieved to the homeland" in the immediate postwar period remained tightly closed to researchers interested in Russian historical and cultural developments in the diaspora. Tragically, too, the facts and whereabouts of their retrieval were likewise concealed or never recorded, even to the extent that trusted Soviet state archivists did not know whence they came. This tragedy begat yet another, as many of these "trophy" materials became subject to theft and dispersal, either en route or due in part to their suspect and incompletely registered status within the archives where they were placed. For example, the so-called "Apostolov Affair" in 1974 involved the theft of more than two hundred early treaties and charters by an employee of the Central State Archive of Early Acts (TsGADA, now RGADA), many of which were subsequently sold on the antiquarian market to collectors in the USSR and abroad. Prosecution of the theft was seriously hampered by the fact that the stolen documents came from "trophy" files, such as early charters and treaties from the Prussian Foreign Ministry Archive that Soviet authorities had from a salt mine in Saxony, and which hence could not be publicly identified with the TsGADA (now RGADA).[60]

POST-STALIN POLITICAL AGENDAS FOR ROSSICA WITH SOVIET FLAVORS

In the decades following the death of Stalin, Soviet archivists were less aggressive in their efforts to acquire foreign archival Rossica and did not have the same opportunities for plunder that presented themselves at the end of the war. An additional Soviet propaganda motive, however, is revealed in the attempt to acquire the papers of Ivan Bunin, to which end, after Bunin's death in Paris, the Soviet Embassy kept in touch with his widow. In 1955 a representative of the Soviet Embassy in Paris gave Vera Bunina a one-time payment of 50,000 francs, presumably in hopes of getting at least part of the Bunin archive. But she suggested she would agree to turn over all of her husband's papers only if they gave her a pension of 70,000 per month. Soviet authorities were concerned because in 1952, a book of Bunin's memoirs of a "White Guard, anti-Soviet character" had been published abroad. Yet in December 1955, CP Central Committee instructions were sent to Paris against a pension. Rather it was deemed important to acquire Bunin's archival materials outright "in order to cure the same reactionary circles of the possibilities of utilizing the undesirable literary heritage of the author for the aims of our enemies."[61] There was no agreement then for Soviet purchase.

Earlier, when the Bunin family was in dire financial straits and Bunin needed yet another operation in Paris, Boris Nikolaevskii (then in New York) served as a broker trying to sell Bunin's papers to Columbia University and at the same time help the founders of the budding Russian Archive. He tried to convince Bunin that his papers would be safer on the other side of the Atlantic. Bunin himself agreed, pending receipt of transport funds and packing assistance; apparently shipping arrangements were negotiated by Simeon Bolan on behalf of Columbia University already by May 1952.[62] From Columbia and other sources, however, we know that Bunin apparently changed his mind at the last moment. The fledgling Russian Archive apparently did not pay enough to satisfy Bunin and his heirs. Yet despite a significant advance and payment for transport, none of the Bunin papers were received in New York.

Soviet authorities continued to follow the fate of the Bunin papers and memorabilia in Paris and were trying to prevent the Bunin papers going to America. After the death of Vera Bunina, the Union of Soviet Writers recommended in 1961, that the Soviet Embassy seek negotiations with the Bunins' heir Leonid Zurov, and "pursue possible arrangements for a two-month pension payment in exchange for the remaining Bunin papers and memorabilia."[63] All the details about the negotiations are not available, but Soviet authorities eventually succeeded in arranging transfer of some Bunin papers to Russia. Those "retrieved" materials are now dispersed between the Russian State Archive of Literature and Art (RGALI) and the Bunin Museum in Orel. However, many of the Bunin papers stayed in Paris with Zurov, then went to Edinburgh, and eventually were donated to the Russian Archive in Leeds. Recently Rosarkhiv has been aggressively protesting that placement, and there has been an outcry in the Russian press. As far as can be determined, however, the collections quite legally reside in Leeds, where a document-level catalogue has recently been published.[64]

The Bunin case was only one of many examples of Soviet attitudes towards the retrieval of archival Rossica. In February 1961 the Soviet writer and literary scholar Iraklii Andronikov addressed the Presidium of the CPSU Central Committee, recommending attention to the Russian documentary heritage abroad. He was particularly concerned that some important literary Rossica, such as the Volkonskii papers, had found their way to American collections because adequate attention and funds were not appropriated for their retrieval to the USSR.[65] A Central Committee reply, however, took issue with Andronikov's recommendation. Glavarkhiv chief Gennadii A. Belov explained that there was "no need to pay attention to all representatives of Russian culture. For example, in view of their inconsequential scientific value, there was no necessity to purchase the personal archives of Merezhkovskii, Gippius, and a series of other emigrants." He was critical of the purchase by

Pushkinskii Dom of the personal archive of Nikolai A. Berdiaev, because such materials "have no relationship whatsoever to Russian culture, nor to A. S. Pushkin and his circles," and hence would "have no interest for Soviet scientific social values."[66]

DESCRIBING ROSSICA ABROAD

During the cold war decades, most retrieved archival Rossica in the USSR were neither described nor available for research use. By contrast, on the other side of the Iron Curtain, descriptive efforts for archival Rossica reached a zenith. The early 1980s, when Soviet archives were closed or highly restricted for Western scholars, saw the publication of a number of major Rossica surveys. To cite only a few examples, Richard Lewanski surveyed Eastern European resources in Western Europe, and Grant and Brown surveyed holdings in the United States and Canada. Later Robert Karlowich's 1990 survey of Russian-related holdings in the New York Metropolitan area also briefly covered the Bakhmeteff holdings, and mentioned the unpublished finding aids, card catalogs, and the RLIN coverage.[67] The survey of archival Rossica in the United Kingdom, compiled almost single-handedly by Janet Hartley, was followed a year later by an impressive catalog of Slavic manuscript books in the UK by Ralph Cleminson.[68]

A decade ago, at a conference in tribute to those publications in London, my suggestion to British scholars that it was important to analyze the provenance of archival Rossica that happened to be found in the United Kingdom in the context of contingent documentation in Soviet archives was viewed as the somewhat unrealistic proposition of an American optimist.[69] Many Russians who today insist that all "Rossica" should be returned to the homeland, and that wide-scale microfilming of Russian archival sources unduly "alienates the heritage of the Fatherland," fail to recognize the extent to which the existence of representative samples of Rossica abroad has encouraged the study and appreciation of Russian history and culture, as was apparent in the London conference.

CONCLUSIONS–
RETRIEVAL OF ROSSICA TODAY WITHOUT RESTITUTION

Today, fortunately, the rationale for and ideology behind Russian efforts in retrieval of archival Rossica contrasts remarkably with the conspiratorial, political propaganda, or imperial efforts of earlier Soviet decades. Yet today the level of patriotic concern that all of the archival legacy of "Russia Abroad" should be retrieved or "repatriated" exists to an extent that often rivals Bonch-Bruevich's aggressive imperial appeal to "leave nothing behind." Beria's aggressive "operational" goals may have been forgotten, but many Russian patriots, political leaders, and archivists today applaud the resulting retrieval of the "archival Rossica" his operations succeeded in repatriating. While they openly applaud the results, they prefer to forget the means. Ironically, even those archives brought to the Soviet Union for "scientific-historical purposes" were long closed for academic research and publication, and many of them are still inadequately described, and thus are only marginally available for research in the "home country."

Often the first reaction of Russian archivists and cultural leaders visiting Houghton Library at Harvard, the Hoover Institution at Stanford, or the Bakhmeteff Archive at Columbia University is one of regret that such rich collections are not in Moscow. They are loath to recognize the foreign collectors' legal rights to materials rescued or purchased, or to thank them for efforts to preserve and describe the exiled archival Rossica. The fall-back Russian position is usually the immediate demand for complete photocopies. Some even suggest that copies should be given to them free of charge–without anything significant in exchange as if they, as Russians, have some inherent right to alienated or exiled manuscripts–"Gimme, it's Russian, it's mine!"

They tend to forget that such archival "Rossica" was often purchased at high price, acquired at considerable risk, or sometimes kept secret to protect the safety of exiles. They do not always understand that once established in an archival home abroad those materials were cared for and described as part of foreign collections, and in most cases are now openly accessible to world scholarship. In some cases the documents were created abroad–Russian, to be sure, but already *émigré* Russian, and in many cases by citizens of the foreign country that had become their home in exile. Such foreign-held Rossica, according to the moral and legal decision of its owners or their heirs, is now subject to property and cultural laws of the new country.

Those interested in Russian history and the international Communist movement should indeed rejoice in the preservation of the Trotsky archives in Houghton Library,[70] in the Hoover Institution,[71] and in the Institute of International Social History in Amsterdam.[72] Similarly, the *Slavic Review* editor rejoiced in the preservation of Mandelstam manuscripts in Princeton University Library, by the conscious choice of Nadezhda Mandelstam.[73] In contrast, in Moscow itself, even in the "new Russia," we still do not know how many Mandelstam manuscripts remain in the former OGPU files. Nor do we know how many fragments of the Trotsky papers were seized abroad by the OGPU, and how many others are now held in the Presidential Archive (AP RF) that remain closed to scholarship to this day.[74]

The opening of the Sakharov Archive in Moscow in May 1994 is symbolic of the new public-spirited democratic concern that repressed and exiled elements in the Russian intellectual tradition be available in Moscow.[75] Other parts of the Sakharov archive have been donated to Brandeis University (Waltham, MA). The Sakharov family has been duly cautious in refusing to turn the materials over to a state archive, and they have not yet returned to Russia the papers that were taken to the West for security in the late 1980s. Such security was appropriate because, as late as 1989, the KGB destroyed "580 volumes of Sakharov materials, [including] Sakharov's diaries."[76] The destruction of Sakharov's files and the continuing lack of open access to Trotsky papers in Russia should cause many émigrés to think twice before transfer of their archives to the homeland.

We should rejoice about the extent to which the Bakhmeteff Archive has insured the preservation of its extensive Rossica collections, provided for their description, and for public access. The efforts of its curators have saved many important materials that otherwise would have been left forgotten in attics, rotting in basements, or even tossed into garbage heaps by those less concerned about the memories and traces of Russia abroad. The availability of such rich collections in New York City has provided the basis for many theses and doctoral dissertation and helped to preserve appreciation of Russian history and culture around the world. We can only hope for further efforts to coordinate the description of Rossica retrieved to the homeland with the archival Rossica that remain abroad, which should be an important goal for foreign collections, such as those we honor today at Columbia University.

LIST OF ABBREVIATIONS AND ACRONYMS

AP RF–*Arkhiv Prezidenta Rossiiskoi Federatsii* (Archive of the President of the Russian Federation)

AVPRI–*Arkhiv vneshnei politiki rossiiskoi imperii* (Archive of Foreign Policy of the Russian Empire)

ERR–*Einsatzstab Reichsleiter Rosenberg* (Special Command of Reichsleiter Rosenberg)

GA RF–*Gosudarstvennyi arkhiv Rossiiskoi Federatsii* (State Archive of the Russian Federation), *formerly* TsGAOR SSSR and TsGA RSFSR

GAU–*Glavnoe arkhivnoe upravlenie*; later also, "Glavarkhiv" (Main Archival Administration)

GIM–*Gosudarstvennyi istoricheskii muzei* (State Historical Museum)

GPU–*Gosudarstvennoe politicheskoe upravlenie* (State Political Administration)

IMEL–*Institut Marksa, Engel'sa i Lenina pri TsK VKP(b)* (Marx, Engels, Lenin Institute under the Central Committee of the All-Russian Communist Party of Bolsheviks), 1931-1954

IML–*Institut Marksizma i Leninizma pri TsK KPSS* (Institute of Marxism Leninism under the Central Committee of the Communist Party of the Soviet Union) 1956-

MGB–*Ministerstvo gosudarstvennoi bezopasnosti* (Ministry of State Security)

MGIAI–*Moskovskii gosudarstvennyi istoriko–arkhivnyi institut* (Moscow State Historico-Archival Institute)

MID–*Ministerstvo inostrannykh del* (Ministry of Foreign Affairs–MFA)

MVD–*Ministerstvo vnutrennikh del* (Ministry of Internal Affairs)

NKVD–*Narodnyi komissariat vnutrennikh del* (People's Commissariat of Internal Affairs)

OGPU–*Ob"edinennoe gosudarstvennoe politicheskoe upravlenie* (Unified State Political Administration)

ORZ–*Otdel literatury Russkogo zarubezh'ia RGB* (Division for Literature of Russia Abroad [Russian State Library])

RGADA–*Rossiiskii gosudarstvennyi arkhiv drevnikh aktov* (Central State Archive of Early Acts), *earlier* TsGADA

RGALI–*Rossiiskii gosudarstvennyi arkhiv literatury i iskusstva* (Russian State Archive of Literature and Art)

RGANI–*Rossiiskii gosudarstvennyi arkhiv noveishei istorii* (Russian State Archive of Contemporary History)

RGASPI–*Rossiiskii gosudarstvennyi arkhiv sotsial'no-politicheskoi istorii* (Russian State Archive of Socio-Political History), *before 1991*, Central Party Archive (TsPA); Russian Center for the Storage and Study of Contemporary History (RTsKhIDNI)

RGB–*Rossiiskaia gosudarstvennaia biblioteka* (Russian State Library), *formerly* the Lenin State Library (GBL)

RSDRP–*Rossiiskaia Sotsial-Demokraticheskaia Rabochaia Partiia* (Russian Social Democratic Workers' Party)

RSHA–*Reichssicherheitshauptamt* (Reich Security Main Office [under the Third Reich])

RZIA–*Russkii zagranichnyi istoricheskii arkhiv* (Russian Foreign Historical Archive, *sometimes* Russian Historical Archive Abroad)

SMERSH–"Smert' shpionam" ("Death to spies" Soviet military counter-intelligence unit)

TsGADA–*Tsentral'nyi gosudarstvennyi arkhiv drevnikh aktov* (Central State Archive of Early Acts), *now* RGADA

TsGAOR–*Tsentral'nyi gosudarstvennyi arkhiv Oktiabrskoi revoliutsii SSSR* (Central State Archive of the October Revolution of the USSR), *since 1992, part of* GA RF

TsKhSD–*Tsentr khraneniia sovremennoi dokumentatsii* (Center for the Preservation of Contemporary Documentation), *now* RGANI

TsPA–*Tsentral'nyi partiinyi arkhiv* (Central Party Archive)

NOTES

1. The Russian word *fond* is used in two basic meanings in this article: fund or foundation; and stock, reserves, or resources.–Ed. (KR).

2. P. K. Grimsted, "Zarubezhnaia arkhivnaia Rossika i Sovetika: problemy proiskhozhdeniia dokumentov i ikh otnoshenie k istorii Rossii (SSSR), potrebnost' v opisanii i bibliografii," *Otechestvennye arkhivy*, 1993, no. 1: 20-53. An expanded English version appeared in Paris, "Archival Rossica/Sovietica Abroad: Provenance or Pertinence, Bibliographic and Descriptive Needs," *Cahiers du Monde Russe et Sovietique* 34, no. 3 (1993): 431-80. Although the term "Rossica" was traditionally used for foreign imprints *about* Russia, it is now being used in Russia with "archival" to denote a wide range of archival materials of Russian "provenance" and "pertinence," as I explain in the articles cited.

3. My longer essay was published in the conference proceedings, "Arkhivnaia Rossika/Sovetika: k opredeleniiu tipologii russkogo arkhivnogo naslediia za rubezhom," in *Problemy zarubezhnoi arkhivnoi Rossiki: sbornik statei*, ed. V. Kozlov (Moscow: "Russkii mir," 1997), 7-43. A variant edition appears in *Trudy Istoriko-arkhivnogo instituta RGGU* 33 (1996): 262-86. See my parallel typology for Ucrainica, "Towards a Descriptive Typology of the Ukrainian Archival Heritage Abroad," in Grimsted, *Trophies of War and Empire: The Archival Heritage of Ukraine, World War II, and the International Politics of Restitution* (Cambridge, MA: Harvard University Press for the Ukrainian Research Institute, 2001), chap. 4, 137-74.

4. See the reflections by Ivan Tolstoi, "Rossiia na Mankhettene: vpechatleniia o konferentsii po Russkomu zarubezh'iu," *Novoe russkoe slovo* (New York), 20-21 October 2001; electronic version at http://chss.irex.ru/db/zarub/view_bib.asp?id=373 (16 June 2003). Below I cite the often erroneous report by Piotr N. Bazanov, "Konferentsiia: 50-let Bakhmetevskogo arkhiva," *Berega* 2002, no. 1: 48-50.

5. I am grateful first to Ellen Scaruffi for alerting me about the "exchange," and more recently to Tanya Chebotarev for searching out relevant data. The quotation from Mosely appears in his reply to Bolan (21 November 1955). Bolan's report on his visit to the Soviet Embassy (9 January 1956) and assurance of a visa to be received in February was dated 23 January 1956. Bolan had been a minor functionary in the imperial Russian Embassy under Boris Bakhmeteff, and was a book dealer in New York during the 1920s and 30s.

6. "Columbia Makes Soviet Book Deal: University Gives up Lenin Letters in Return for Rare Bibliographical Items," special to *The New York Times* (Moscow, 30 May), printed in the issue of 7 June 1956. I am grateful to Edward Kasinec for sending

me a copy. For example, Tanya Chebotarev verified that the original Vereshchagin albums and the Lermontov manuscript remain in the Columbia safe. Bolan had suggested to Moseley offering copies of those in his letter listing proposed items for exchange (15 November 1955), and apparently that was what he did.

7. Leonid K. Vinogradov, "Popolnenie fondov Tsentral'nogo partiinogo arkhiva," *Voprosy istorii KPSS*, 1958, no. 2: 217.

8. Leonid K. Vinogradov, "Posleslovie," in Roman Peresvetov, *Poiski bestsennogo naslediia: o sud'be nekotorykh rukopisei V. I. Lenina*, 2d ed. (Moskva: Politizdat, 1968), 325. A copy of the transfer paper from Columbia or report about Bolan's trip has not been located.

9. Vinogradov, in Peresvetov, *Poiski bestsennogo naslediia*, 324-25.

10. *Fond dokumentov V. I. Lenina*, 2d ed. (Moskva: Izd-vo politicheskoi literatury, 1984), 143-44. The first edition appeared in 1970. The Columbia card catalog lists it as a "broadside in verse in the hand of Lenin" ["Byl burnyi god. . ."], (n.p., [1907]); the original remains in the safe.

11. Vinogradov, in Peresvetov, *Poiski bestsennogo naslediia*, 324-25.

12. Aleksinskii to Magerovsky, 7 September 1965, as confirmed to me by the Bakhmeteff Archive. The letter suggests that he hoped for Moseley's visit to Paris, presumably to discuss the disposition of his library and archive (more than thirty crates).

13. *Fond dokumentov V. I. Lenina*, 153. The letter from Lenin to Aleksinskii (7 February 1908) is published in its entirety in *V. I Lenin: neizvestnye dokumenty, 1891-1922*, comp. and ed. Iu. N. Amiantov et al. (Moskva: ROSSPEN, 1999), 27-28 (no. 10).

14. The quotation comes from "Vypiska iz protokola No 112 §IIs Sekretariata TsK," 5 February 1974, 4/22/1236, folio 88, Russian State Archive of Contemporary History (RGANI), with indication that the extract had been sent to Comrades [Iurii] Andropov and [Ekaterina] Furtseva. This document was first quoted at the 1993 Rosarkhiv conference by TsKhSD (now RGANI) archivist A. M. Petrov, "Voprosy vozvrashcheniia arkhivnoi Rossiki v dokumentakh TsK KPSS: 1953-1986 gg.," in *Problemy zarubezhnoi arkhivnoi Rossiki*, 175. I appreciate Petrov's showing me his report prior to publication and TsKhSD for a copy of the original. Further details of the "exchange" are not available, and Petrov had not determined where it took place.

15. Bakhmeteff Curator Tanya Chebotarev assures me the February 1908 letter was not on the acquisition inventory for the Aleksinskii collection. (The Bakhmeteff Archive has only a typescript copy of a Lenin letter to Aleksinskii dated 3 February 1908.) The undated [1908] letter in the small part of the Aleksinskii Collection at Harvard is described in the detailed, annotated finding aid–"bMS Russ 73 Aleksinskii, Grigorii, b. 1879, Papers: Guide" (Cambridge MA: Houghton Library, Harvard College Library), available electronically at: http://oasis.harvard.edu.html/hou00147.html (16 June 2003).

16. Steven A. Grant and John H. Brown, eds., *The Russian Empire and Soviet Union: A Guide to Manuscripts and Archival Materials in the United States* (Boston: G.K. Hall, 1981), 298-343.

17. Aleksandr D. Stepanskii, "Rossiiskie dokumenty v arkhivakh N'iu-Iorka," *Otechestvennye arkhivy*, 1992, no. 3: 117-19.

18. See the interview of Vladimir Kozlov with Ella Maksimova, "Sokrovishcha Rossii rasseiany po miru–kak ikh vernut'?" *Izvestiia,* 16 February 1994, 7.

19. Elliot Mossman, "From the Editor," *Slavic Review* 55, no. 1 (Spring 1994): [ix-x]. In translation, it appears more appropriate to use the term "archival-information 'sphere.' "

20. Vladimir Kozlov, "Vyiavlenie i vozvrashchenie zarubezhnoi arkhivnoi Rossiki: opyt i perspektivy," *Vestnik arkhivista*, 1993, no. 6(18): 11-27; see also the more finished version in *Novaia i noveishaia istoriia,* 1994, no. 3: 13-23. Both versions were followed by "Rekomendatsii nauchno-prakticheskoi konferentsii 'Problemy zarubezhnoi arkhivnoi Rossiki,' 21-22 dekabria 1993 g." Many of the participants are listed in the preceding report (9-10). See also the report of the conference organizer, Elena E. Novikova, "O rabote rossiiskikh arkhivistov po vyiavleniiu i vozvrashcheniiu arkhivnoi Rossiki," in *Problemy zarubezhnoi arkhivnoi Rossiki,* especially 44-47.

21. See also the bibliography of Russian archival legislation in *Archives in Russia: A Directory and Bibliographic Guide to Repositories in Moscow and St. Petersburg* (Armonk, NY: M.E. Sharpe, 2000).

22. Budnik's presentation to the 1993 conference, however, was not published in the conference proceedings.

23. See the parliamentary discussion to this effect in Federal'noe Sobranie, Parlament Rossiiskoi Federatsii, *Biulleten',* no. 34, *Zasedaniia Gosudarstvennoi Dumy, 20 maia 1994 goda* (Moscow, 1994), 31-32.

24. The Belov letter to the Central Committee (2 July 1965), was found in RGANI, 5/35/212, folios 158-159. The incident was first mentioned by Petrov at the 1993 Rosarkhiv conference–"Voprosy vozvrashcheniia arkhivnoi Rossiki," 174. I provide more documentation about the Soviet refusal of the American 1965 restitution offer here, because in an unsubstantiated criticism of my oral presentation in New York, Russian participant Piotr Bazanov, "Konferentsiia: 50-let Bakhmetevskogo arkhiva," *Berega*, 2002, no. 1: 49, claimed that "such a precedent never took place."

25. See more details in Grimsted, *The Odyssey of the Smolensk Party Archive: Communist Party Archives for the Service of Anti-Communism*, Carl Beck Papers in Russian & East European Studies, no. 1201 (Pittsburgh PA: University of Pittsburgh, Center for Russian and East European Studies, 1995), especially 80-88.

26. Among the press coverage of the return of the "Smolensk Archive," see Celestine Bohlen, "A Stray Record of Stalinist Horrors Finds Its Way Home," *The New York Times*, 14 December 2002, A21.

27. See Grimsted, "Russia's Trophy Archives: Still Prisoners of World War II?" [Online]. Budapest: Open Society Archive (Central European University), last revised March 2002. Available: http://www.osa.ceu.hu/publications/2002/RussianTrophyArchives/RussianTrophyArchives.html (16 June 2003).

28. See the transcript of the Duma session of 13 June 1996 (59), and the official "Postanovlenie Gosudarstvennoi Dumy–Ob obmene arkhivnykh dokumentov Kniazheskogo doma Likhtenshtein, peremeshchennykh posle okonchaniia Vtoroi mirovoi voiny na territoriiu Rossii, na arkhivnye dokumenty o rassledovanii obstoiatel'stv gibeli Nikolaia II i chlenov ego sem'i: arkhiv N. A. Sokolova," 13 June 1996 (No. 465–II GD). The Rothschild "exchange" and others are discussed in Grimsted, "Russia's Trophy Archives."

29. See further discussion of the Rosarkhiv-Hoover agreement in the context of Russian public reaction, in Grimsted, "Russian Archives in Transition: Caught between Political Crossfire and Economic Crisis," *American Archivist* 55 (Fall 1993): 614-62. Regarding the termination, see Grimsted, *Archives in Russia Seven Years After: "Purveyors of Sensations" or "Shadows Cast out to the Past,"* Working Paper, no. 20, Washington, DC: Cold War International History Project, 1998. Also available on the Internet: http://wwics.si.edu/topics/pubs/ACF518.pdf (part 1) and http://wwics.si.edu/topics/pubs/ACF51B.pdf (part 2) (16 June 2003).

30. See the published guides to RTsKhIDNI (now RGASPI) for a complete listing of foreign collections in original and microform copy that were brought together at TsPA during the Soviet regime. Only in a few cases are details about their provenance provided.

31. Peresvetov, *Poiski bestsennogo naslediia*.

32. "Lenin Documents Abroad," chap. 2, sec. 4 of *Fond dokumentov V. I. Lenina* (*Fond* of V. I. Lenin Documents), 2d ed. (Moscow: Izd-vo politicheskoi literatury, 1984), 134-165.

33. A. Petrov, "Voprosy vozvrashcheniia arkhivnoi Rossiki," p. 175-176, described this incident involving Lenin letters dated 11 August 1909 and 6 July 1911. I was not able to acquire a copy of that document and Petrov does not mention to whom the Lenin letters were addressed. Efforts are underway to document the transfer of those paintings abroad, reported through an agent in Germany.

34. Dmitrii Volkogonov refers to the 1936 seizure in Paris in *Trotsky: The Eternal Revolutionary*, trans. and ed. Harold Shukman (New York: The Free Press, 1996), 371.

35. See E. I. Sokolova's report from the 1993 Rosarkhiv conference, "Iz istorii vozvrashcheniia arkhivnoi Rossiki v 1930-e gg.: po materialam lichnogo fonda V. D. Bonch-Bruevicha," (From the History of the Return of Archival Rossica in the 1930s: According to Materials in the Personal Fond of V. D. Bonch-Bruevich), in *Problemy zarubezhnoi arkhivnoi Rossiki*, 165-69. See also the earlier article by V. A. Chernykh, "Bonch-Bruevich i poluchenie iz-za granitsy rukopisnykh materialov po istorii russkoi kul'tury" (Bonch-Bruevich and the Receipt of Manuscript Materials on the History of Russian Culture From Abroad), *Arkheograficheskii ezhegodnik za 1973 god* (Moscow, 1974), 133-46. Chernykh used mainly sources in RGALI (then TsGALI) and did apparently not have access to the materials in the Lenin Library cited by Sokolova and that I cite below. See also the report of K. G. Mezhova, "Protokoly zasedanii fondovoi komissii kak istochnik po istorii komplektovaniia rukopisnykh fondov Gosudarstvennogo literaturnogo muzeia v Moskve," *Arkheograficheskii ezhegodnik za 1973 god*, 147-55.

36. Bonch-Bruevich to Stalin, 5 July 1935, 369/206/10, folio 47-47v (signed typewritten copy), Russian State Library, Manuscript Division.

37. Bonch-Bruevich to Stalin, 24 February 1945, *fond* 71/125, file 308, folios 2-8; the long quote is from folio 3, RGASPI.

38. Bonch-Bruevich to Stalin, folios 3, 6, 7-8.

39. Chernytsov to Molotov, 22 June 1945, 5325/2/1353, fol. 51, GA RF. The *Pravda* announcement appeared as "Dar Akademii nauk SSSR ot chekhoslovatskogo pravitel'stva" (Tass, 17 June 1945), *Pravda*, 18 June 1945. The first Russian scholarly published account underplayed that aspect of the retrieval–see T. F. Pavlova, "Russkii zagranichnyi istoricheskii arkhiv v Prage," *Voprosy istorii*, 1990, no. 11, 19-30. See also the 1990 interview by Natal'ia Davydova with Moscow State Historico-Archival Institute (MGIAI) specialist Valerii Sedel'nikov, "Arkhiv, o kotorom dolgo molchali," (Archive About Which They Long Kept Silent) *Moskovskie novosti*, 15 April 1990, 16.

40. See more details about the transfer of RZIA and UIK and the fate of the retrieved materials in Kyiv in Grimsted, *Trophies of War and Empire*, Chap. 9, 330-88.

41. Sergei Kruglov to Stalin, 9401/2/134, folios 1-2, GA RF. Details about its arrival in Moscow under tight security and its immediate transfer to TsGAOR SSSR appear in a report dated 3 January 1946, among Glavarkhiv records in 5325/10/2023, GA RF. Nikitinskii's receipt on behalf of TsGAOR SSSR (2 January 1946), is found in 5326/2/1705A, GA RF. The official receipt by the Academy of Sciences (dated 3

January 1946) was signed slightly later, Vavilov to Nikitinskii, 31 January 1946, 5325/10/2023, folio 40, GA RF.

42. Sergei Kruglov to Zhdanov, 15 May 1946, *fond* 5325 (Glavarkhiv)/10/2023, folio 46, GA RF (formerly TsGAOR SSSR).

43. A series of reports on the work of the archive during 1946 are found in the same file among Glavarkhiv records (5325/2/1791, GA RF)–for example, Gur'ianov and Golikova to Nikitinskii, 15 October 1946, folios 8-18; Golikova to Starov, 27 October 1946, folios 19-20; Prokopenko to Kuz'min, 25 November 1946, folio 23, and to Starov, 23 December 1946, folio 24.

44. Sergei Postnikov survived imprisonment, but died soon after his release; the librarians Petr Bovrovskii and Nikolai Tsvetkov perished in a Soviet prison, as explained by Vladimir Bystrov, "Konets Russkogo zagranichnogo istoricheskogo arkhiva v Prage" (The End of the Russian Historical Archive Abroad in Prague), in *Mezhdunarodnaia konferentsiia "Russkaia, ukrainskaia i belorusskaia emigratsiia v Chekhoslovakii mezhdu dvumia mirovymi voinami: rezul'taty i perspektivy issledovanii: fondy Slavianskoi biblioteki i prazhskikh arkhivov," Praga, 14-15 avgusta 1995 g.: sbornik dokladov* (Prague, 1995), vol. 1, 79-80.

45. A printed guide was prepared for the RZIA and many of the other émigré materials in TsGAOR SSSR as a second volume of the TsGAOR *Putevoditel'* (Guide) (Moscow, 1952; GAU); its secret classification was not lifted until 1987, and by then there were only a very few copies extant, one of which has been available in the GA RF reading room.

46. See T. F. Pavlova, ed., *Mezharkhivnyi putevoditel' Russkogo zagranichnogo istoricheskogo arkhiva* (Moscow: ROSSPEN, 1999). I commented accordingly at the official presentation of the guide, symbolically held in the auditorium of the former TsPA (now RGASPI).

47. Susaikov to Kruglov, Bucharest, 19 May 1945, 5325/2/992, folios 209-210, GA RF. The materials were received officially in Moscow by a receipt dated 10 May 1945, folio 207.

48. Istomin and A. Iur'ev to E. I. Golubtsov, 19 May 1945, 5325/2/992, folio 205, GA RF.

49. Reports of the transfer of these materials from Sofia have not yet been located, although there are several published Russian references.

50. I. I. Nikitinskii to Kruglov, 31 May 1947, 5325/2/2172, folios 2, 5, and 7, GA RF.

51. See M. B. Falaleeva, "Fond Romanovykh v sobranii OPI GIM," *Arkheograficheskii ezhegodnik za 1996 god* (Moscow, 1998), especially 270-81.

52. Bakhmutov to Nikitinskii, 5 January 1945, 5325/2/1705, folio 4, and subsequent documents, folios 5, 8-9, and 11-15, GA RF, which provide more details about the materials retrieved from Manchuria.

53. The castle is about 100 kilometers south of Breslau (now Polish Wrocław), near the Czech border. Kobulov to Beria, 27 November 1945, 5325/10/2027, folios 9-10 (cc folios 11-12), GA RF. See Beria's order to Kobulov in red pencil on the first copy, and Kobulov to Selivanovskii, 29 November 1945, folio 13. At least seven wagons had first been sent to Kyiv, but on Beria's personal order were transferred to Moscow; thirteen railroad cars arrived from Kyiv in October 1945, and fifteen were sent to Moscow directly in November (5325/10/2027, folios 14-20, GA RF).

54. See more details about the RSHA collecting operations, Soviet seizure, and subsequent disposition of many of the materials in Grimsted, "Twice Plundered or

'Twice Saved': Identifying Russia's 'Trophy' Archives Amidst the Loot of the Reichssicherheitshauptamt," *Holocaust and Genocide Studies* 15, no. 2 (2001), 191-244. A Russian edition is in preparation.

55. Regarding the seizure of the Paris Slavic libraries in Autumn 1940 and their wartime and postwar fate, see Grimsted, "Twice Plundered, but Still Not Home from the War: The Fate of Three Slavic Libraries Confiscated by the Nazis from Paris," *Solanus* 16 (2002): 39-76. See also Grimsted, "The Odyssey of the Petliura Library from Paris and the Records of the Ukrainian National Republic during World War II," *Harvard Ukrainian Studies* 22 (1998): 181-208 [=Zvi Gitelman et al., eds., *Cultures and Nations of Central and Eastern Europe: Essays in Honor of Roman Szporluk*]; and "The Postwar Fate of the Petliura Library and the Records of the Ukrainian National Republic," *Harvard Ukrainian Studies* 21 (1997 [2001]): 393-461.

56. See the printed versions: Nadezhda V. Ryzhak, "Kollektsiia parizhskoi Russkoi obshchestvennoi biblioteki im. I. S. Turgeneva v fondakh RGB," in *Rumiantsevskie chteniia 2002: Natsional'naia biblioteka v sovremennom sotsiokul'turnom protsesse,* vol. 1: *Tezisy i soobshcheniia* (Moscow: RGB, 2002), 296-301; and Valeriia S. Miasishcheva, "Ob opyte raboty s inostrannymi knizhnymi kollektsiiami, popavshimi v SSSR v sostave kul'turnykh tsennostei, peremeshchennykh v rezul'tate Vtoroi mirovoi voiny i nakhodiashchikhsia v Otdele khraneniia osnovnykh fondov: v kontekste deiatel'nosti po raskrytiiu knizhnykh fondov za starye gody," *Rumiantsevskie chteniia 2002,* vol. 1, 280-83. See also Ryzhak and Miasishcheva, "Vtoraia mirovaia voina i sud'ba izdanii parizhskoi Turgenevskoi biblioteki, okazavshikhsia v RGB," *Bibliotekovedenie,* 2002, no. 5, 104-108.

57. See my monograph, *Books as Victims and Trophies of War: The Odyssey of the Turgenev Library from Paris, 1940-2002* (Amsterdam: International Institute of Social History, forthcoming). As described in more detail in that study, the administrative archives of the Turgenev Library are now dispersed in GA RF, *fonds* R-6846 and R-6162; RGASPI, *fond* 2, *opis'* 1, nos. 25573 and 26073; and RGB Manuscript Division, *fond* 868. I provide details here because a Russian commentator on the Columbia University conference accused me of falsification in connection with my brief mention of the fate of the Turgenev Library in my oral presentation in New York–P. Bazanov, "Konferentsiia: 50-let Bakhmetevskogo arkhiva," *Berega*, 2002, no. 1: 49.

58. The existence of the LaSalle collection in TsPA was officially admitted in an openly published article in 1990–Valerii N. Shepelev, "Tsentral'nyi partiinyi arkhiv otkryvaet svoi fondy: informatsiia dlia issledovatelia," (TsPA Opens Its Collections: Information for the Researcher), *Sovetskie arkhivy,* 1990, no. 4: 19-31. Detailed finding aids for the LaSalle collection had been prepared in Germany before the war. During an interview in July 1991, Ivan N. Kitaev, then IML deputy director and director of TsPA, assured me that no other captured or "trophy" records were held in TsPA, but subsequent research has proved there are many.

59. See the [1993] Chadwyck-Healey advertising brochure for the microform collection *Leaders of the Russian Revolution*, which mentions that the Trotskii papers include "Trotsky's dossier compiled by the French Ministry of War."

60. Rom Petrov and Andrei Chernyi, "Poteriavshi–plachem," (Lost, With Tears), *Ogonek*, 1990, no. 9: 9-11.

61. B. Riurikov, Deputy Head of the Cultural Department of the CPSU Central Committee, and V. Ivanov, Section Head, to Central Committee of Communist Party of the Soviet Union, 7 December 1955, 5/17/535, folio 124, RGANI.

62. The negotiations are apparent in the copies of several of Nikolaevskii's letters to Bunin (New York, 21 July 1948 and 12 January 1952). In a letter from Bunin to Nikolaevskii (Paris, 24 May 1952), he clearly agreed to the transfer if someone would come and do the packing, "because he was too weak." But in a note to Moseley (4 June 1952), Nikolaevskii emphasized Bunin's terminal illness and the family's need to sell the papers. Papers of I. A. Bunin, box 268, folder 7, Boris Nicolaevsky Collection, series 207, Hoover Institution of War, Revolution, and Peace. According to documentation in the Russian Archive, Columbia paid an advance but never received any papers from Bunin.

63. This is explained in a letter of K. Voronkov, Secretary of the Board of the Union of Soviet Writers to the CPSU Central Committee, (3 July 1961), and a memorandum of D. Polikarpov to the Central Committee, 7 July 1961, 5/36/133, folios 177-179, RGANI. There is no indication whether or not the pension was paid or how much.

64. The papers were bequeathed first to Leonid F. Zurov, and subsequently to Dr. D. E. Green of Edinburgh, who later donated them to the Leeds Russian Archive. Regarding the negotiations for the disposition of the Bunin papers, see the introduction to the admirable new finding aid compiled by Anthony J. Heywood, *Catalogue of the Bunin, Bunina, Zurov and Lopatina Collections* (Leeds: Leeds University Press, 2000); the author was not, however, aware of the Central Committee documentation or the Nikolaevskii documentation in Hoover cited above. Richard Davies kindly furnished me copies of many virulent recent articles from the Russian press demanding repatriation of the Bunin papers, but Leeds claims legal rights and intends to respect the terms of bequest of the Bunin heirs.

65. I. L. Andronikov to the Presidium of the CPSU Central Committee, 8 February 1961, 5/36/133, folios 128-133, RGANI.

66. G. A. Belov to the Presidium of the CPSU Central Committee, 5/36/133, folios 134-138, RGANI. See Petrov, "Voprosy vozvrashcheniia arkhivnoi Rossiki," 171-73.

67. All of these directories and others are described in Grimsted, "Archival Rossica/Sovietica Abroad," *Cahiers du Monde Russe et Soviétique* 34, no. 3 (July-September 1993), 453-59.

68. The Hartley directory was deservedly appreciated in a report at the 1993 Moscow conference, although the author assumed it was the work of a large "team of historians and archivists," which was hardly the case–D. A. Gutnov, "Obzor dokumentov po istorii Rossii v arkhivakh Velikobritanii" (Review of Documents on the History of Russia in British Archives), *Problemy zarubezhnoi arkhivnoi Rossiki*, 100-106.

69. Grimsted, "Foreign Collections and Soviet Archives: Russian Archeographic Efforts in Great Britain and the Problem of Provenance," in *The Study of Russian History from British Archival Sources*, 173-84.

70. Regarding the Trotskii Archive at Harvard, see Jvan Heijenoort, "The History of Trotsky's Papers," *Harvard Library Bulletin*, 1980: 191-98, and the detailed typescript inventory, "Guide to the Papers of Leon Trotsky and Related Collections in the Harvard College Library," 2d version (Cambridge, 1959). Series-level listings are available online in the RLIN database.

71. The largest group of Trotsky papers at Hoover (intermixed with those of Lev L'vovich Sedov), are described in Anna M. Bourguina and Michael Jakobson, comps., *Guide to the Boris I. Nicolaevsky Collection in the Hoover Institution Archives*, Part I (Stanford: Hoover Institution Press, 1989), sec. 231, 224-350, although there is scattered documentation from and relating to Trotsksy in other parts of the Nicolaevsky Collection and other collections in the Hoover Archives.

72. See the brief reference to the Trotskii papers in Atie van der Horst and Elly Koen, eds., *Guide to the International Archives and Collections at the International Institute of Social History, Amsterdam* (Amsterdam: IISH, 1989), 164-65, and the more detailed typewritten inventory available in IISH.

73. Mossman, "From the Editor," [ix-x].

74. Regarding the severe restrictions remaining for the Archive of the President of the Russian Federation (AP RF), see the newspaper article by Ella Maksimova, "Prodavtsy sensatsii iz Arkhiva Presidenta," (Sellers of Sensation from the Archive of the President), *Izvestiia*, 13 July 1994, 5. Regarding the Trotskii materials there, see also the comment in reply by Dmitrii Volkogonov, "Nel'zia vo vsem videt' zloi umysel," *Izvestiia*, 19 July 1994, 5. Even General Dmitrii Volkogonov admitted that his recent study of Trotskii was based on the materials in Cambridge and Amsterdam, and he had only minimal access to Trotskii documents held in Moscow–*Trotsky*, xxxiv.

75. A parallel English-Russian brochure describing the Sakharov Archive was issued in honor of the opening, *Arkhhiv Sakharova v Moskve* (Moscow, 1994).

76. Interview with Vadim Bakatin, *Literaturnaia gazeta*, 18 December 1991 (English translation in *Foreign Broadcast Information Service*–FBIS–SOV-91-249, 27 December 1991.) Contrary to some speculation, the family was not given copies of the files that were destroyed.

SPECIAL 25%-OFF DISCOUNT!

Order a copy of this book with this form or online at:
http://www.haworthpress.com/store/product.asp?sku=5133
Use Sale Code BOF25 in the online bookshop to receive 25% off!

RUSSIAN AND EAST EUROPEAN BOOKS AND MANUSCRIPTS IN THE UNITED STATES

*Proceedings of a Conference in Honor of the Fiftieth Anniversary
of the Bakhmeteff Archive of Russian and East European History and Culture*

____ in softbound at $14.96 (regularly $19.95) (ISBN: 0-7890-2405-5)
____ in hardbound at $29.96 (regularly $39.95) (ISBN: 0-7890-2404-7)

COST OF BOOKS _____

Outside USA/ Canada/
Mexico: Add 20% _____

POSTAGE & HANDLING _____
(US: $4.00 for first book & $1.50
for each additional book)
Outside US: $5.00 for first book
& $2.00 for each additional book)

SUBTOTAL _____

in Canada: add 7% GST _____

STATE TAX _____
(NY, OH, & MIN residents please
add appropriate local sales tax

FINAL TOTAL _____
(if paying in Canadian funds, convert
using the current exchange rate,
UNESCO coupons welcome)

❏ **BILL ME LATER:** ($5 service charge will be added)
(Bill-me option is good on US/Canada/
Mexico orders only; not good to jobbers,
wholesalers, or subscription agencies.)

❏ **Signature** _____

❏ **Payment Enclosed: $** _____

❏ **PLEASE CHARGE TO MY CREDIT CARD:**

❏ Visa ❏ MasterCard ❏ AmEx ❏ Discover
❏ Diner's Club ❏ Eurocard ❏ JCB

Account #_____

Exp Date _____

Signature_____
*(Prices in US dollars and subject to
change without notice.)*

PLEASE PRINT ALL INFORMATION OR ATTACH YOUR BUSINESS CARD

Name		
Address		
City	State/Province	Zip/Postal Code
Country		
Tel		Fax
E-Mail		

May we use your e-mail address for confirmations and other types of information? ❏Yes ❏No
We appreciate receiving your e-mail address. Haworth would like to e-mail special discount
offers to you, as a preferred customer. **We will never share, rent, or exchange your e-mail
address.** We regard such actions as an invasion of your privacy.

Order From Your Local Bookstore or Directly From
The Haworth Press, Inc.
10 Alice Street, Binghamton, New York 13904-1580 • USA
Call Our toll-free number (1-800-429-6784) / Outside US/Canada: (607) 722-5857
Fax: 1-800-895-0582 / Outside US/Canada: (607) 771-0012
E-Mail your order to us: Orders@haworthpress.com

Please Photocopy this form for your personal use.
www.HaworthPress.com

BOF03